The Plot To Kill God

EDWARD F. MRKVICKA, JR.
WITH KELLY H. MRKVICKA

outskirtspress
DENVER, COLORADO

The Plot To Kill God
All Rights Reserved.
Copyright © 2015 Edward F. Mrkvicka, Jr. with Kelly H. Mrkvicka
v5.0

Cover Photo © 2015 thinkstockphotos.com. All rights reserved - used with permission.

Outskirts Press, Inc.
http://www.outskirtspress.com

ISBN: 978-1-4787-4572-3

Outskirts Press and the "OP" logo are trademarks belonging to Outskirts Press, Inc.

PRINTED IN THE UNITED STATES OF AMERICA

CONTENTS

PREFACE
THE PARABLE OF THE MADMAN

THE MADMAN—Have you not heard of that madman, who lit a lantern in the bright morning hours, ran to the market place and cried incessantly: "I seek God! I seek God!"

—As many of those, who did not believe in God were standing around just then, he provoked much laughter.

"Has he gotten lost?" asked one.

"Did he lose his way like a child?" asked another.

"Or is he hiding? Is he afraid of us? Has he gone on a voyage? Emigrated?"— Thus they yelled and laughed.

The madman jumped into their midst and pierced them with his eyes. "Whither is God?" he cried. "I will tell you. *We have killed him—* you and I. All of us are his murderers. But how did we do this? How could we drink up the sea? Who gave us the sponge to wipe away the entire horizon? What were we doing when we unchained this earth from its sun? Whither is it moving now? Whither are we moving? Away from all suns? Are we not plunging continually? Backward, sideward, forward, in all directions? Is there still any *up* or *down*? Are we not straying, as through an infinite nothing? Do we not feel the breath of empty space? Has it not become colder? Is not night continually closing in on us? Do we not need to light lanterns in the morning? Do we hear nothing as yet of the noise of the gravediggers, who are burying God? Do we smell nothing as yet of the divine decomposition? Gods, too, decompose. God is dead. God remains dead. And we have killed him."

"How shall we comfort ourselves, the murderers of all murderers? What was holiest and mightiest of all that the world has yet owned has bled to death under our knives. Who will wipe this blood off us? What water is there for us to clean ourselves? What festivals of atonement, what sacred games shall we have to invent? Is not the greatness of this deed too great for us? Must we ourselves not become gods simply to appear worthy of it? There has never been a greater deed; and whoever is born after us—for the sake of this deed he will belong to a higher history than all history hitherto."

Here the madman fell silent and looked again at his listeners; and they, too, were silent and stared at him in astonishment. At last he threw his lantern on the ground, and it broke into pieces and went out.

"I have come too early," he said then. "My time is not yet. This tremendous event is still on its way, still wandering; it has not yet reached the ears of men. Lightning and thunder require time; the light of the stars requires time; deeds, though done, still require time. To be seen and heard. This deed is still more distant from them than the most distant stars—*and yet they have done it themselves.*"

It has been related further that on the same day the madman forced his way into several churches and there struck up his *requiem aeternam deo.* Led out and called to account, he is said always to have replied nothing but: "What, after all, are these churches now if they are not the tombs and sepulchers of God?"

Source: Friedrich Nietzsche, *The Gay Science* (1882, 1887) para. 125; Walter Kaufmann ed. (New York: Vintage, 1974), pp.181-82.

INTRODUCTION

Many moments in history have changed the course of man: the rise and fall of the Roman Empire, World War I, the discovery of penicillin, World War II, nuclear weaponry, the polio vaccine, and man walking on the moon. Other defining moments, while it's not possible to list them all—they all have one thing in common: from that moment forward, things dramatically changed.

My maternal grandmother lived to be 97. In her lifetime she saw settlers traveling west in Conestoga wagons, the implanting of an artificial heart, and a man walking on the moon. She wasn't so much impressed by the events themselves, but that so many huge events could occur in the lifetime of one person.

She was right, as it has been estimated that 90 % of man's progress in technology has occurred within the last 50 years. That's almost too much to comprehend. It also makes a person wonder about the next 50 years.

I'm not a history buff per se, but I am fascinated by the overall concept espoused by 19th century American novelist George Santayana: "Those who will not learn from history are doomed to repeat it." That's worthy of deep reflection, because we can no longer continue to repeat our mistakes. For example, wars from the dawn of time to approximately 80 years ago have always been devastating, but recoverable. For example, the Civil War did not endanger the planet and/or man as an entity. However, a next war that includes nuclear weapons will exact a great price. The planet and mankind may be destroyed. We must learn from history to avoid that which must be avoided.

Another example: we are no longer protected by natural physical barriers, such as the oceans. So when a new disease strikes in one part of the world, thanks to intercontinental air travel, it's only days before the disease can be on the other side of the planet. Diseases used to be isolated. They are no longer.

Then there is man's arrogance and lack of medical ethics. Simply put, just because man can do things never before imagined doesn't mean he should. At some point, it is highly possible we are going to open a can of worms that will wipe man out quickly.

As bad as these few scenarios and others are, I am writing this book to say to the world that we are in the process of doing something far more devastating than employing nuclear weapons or unleashing a biological disaster, something so horrendous we will not survive on any level. And we will accomplish this "goal" with a smile on our faces and joy in our hearts, all the while believing we are doing the right thing.

It begins and ends with the killing of God.

1

WHO IS THIS GOD
WHO MUST BE KILLED?

It is essential in any relationship that each person has a working knowledge of the other. Of course, there are varying degrees. We don't have to know much about a clerk at the shopping mall. At the other end of the spectrum is a spouse. If we are going to have successful marriages, we must come to know our mates intimately.

In our personal relationships we work hard to understand one another, to communicate effectively, to have a life together. But we almost universally ignore tending our most important relationship--the relationship with the One who created us. He knows us, but we too often only know Him according to our wants and needs, and not as He truly is. The Bible reveals the truth about our God.

God is Love

At every opportunity I ask my brothers and sisters in Christ, "Who is God?"

Without exception I receive an answer like "God is love." And, of course, that answer is correct: God is love.

He that loveth not, knoweth not God; for God is love.
(1 John 4:8)

And how deep is that love?

Greater love has no one than this, than to lay down one's life
for his friends.
(John 15:13)

But if that's all we know, if that's all we see, if that's all we feel, we
have diminished His divine character to the point of being unrecognizable and unworthy of worship. Saying "God is love" and leaving it
at that is akin to saying the Sistine Chapel ceiling is painted, and the
Freedom Tower is a building. And therein lies a danger.

It's analogous to telling a small child not to play in the street because if he falls he might skin his knee on the concrete. It also might
be wise to explain that if he plays in the street he may get run over by
a 3,500 pound car. Cliffs Notes are fine if you simply want to write
a novel about surgery, but if you're actually going to perform surgery
you'll have to expand your depth of study.

The reason believers give the simplistic answer that "God is love"
is due to the fact that many Christians worship a divided Christ. That
is—many of us accept Christ as our personal Savior, but our disobedience reveals we reject Him as our Lord.

We fail to obey Him because we don't truly know Him in all his
glory.

Also, some churches have begun to tailor the Gospel to compromise with the world. Too many people come to church solely to be
emotionally uplifted, not to worship. Church has, to some, become a
weekly spiritual comfort-stop where one doesn't want to be burdened
with uncomfortable sermons about sin, hell, or adultery. No, we want
our consciences soothed, regardless of the fruits of our sins. To accomplish that goal precludes accepting the Gospel as it is written. Settling
for a soothed conscience precludes accepting the Gospel as it is written
and keeps us from knowing Jesus as Savior and Lord.

But there were also false prophets among the people, even as

there will be false teachers among you, who will secretly bring in destructive heresies, even denying the Lord who bought them, [and] bring on themselves swift destruction. And many will follow their destructive ways, because of whom the way of truth will be blasphemed.
(2 Peter 2:11)

God is Intelligent Beyond Imagination

God is love, but He is also intelligent beyond human comprehension. He created the heavens and the earth in a day.

This [is] the history of the heavens and the earth when they were created, in the day that the LORD God made the earth and the heavens.
(Genesis 2:4)

He knows the whereabouts of everyone in the world, what they are doing, and what they are thinking every single second of every single day. He knows everyone who has gone before. He is to us a trillion times over what Einstein's intelligence was to a single-cell life form. If we think, even subconsciously, that we can debate, out-maneuver, or make a deal with Him, we are deluding ourselves.

Search me, O God, and know my heart; Try me, and know my anxieties; And see if [there is any] wicked way in me, And lead me in the way everlasting.
(Psalm 139:23-24)

Nor can we continue in our sin and be secure in the knowledge that by repenting at some later date we'll be forgiven. One of Satan's most successful strategies has been to convince people there's always tomorrow, that God can wait. But He can't--He won't. You cannot openly sin while believing you'll repent later, but before you die.

"In an acceptable time I have heard you, And in the day of salvation I have helped you. Behold, now [is] the accepted time; behold, now [is] the day of salvation."
(2 Corinthians 6:2)

"Today, if you will hear His voice, Do not harden your hearts as in the rebellion."
(Hebrews 3:15)

So while we may intend to eventually get around to seeing things God's way, He, having given warning, may decide that our last day on earth is today whether we're ready or not. Procrastination in responding to God's love is a direct result of people not knowing the God we say we love.

God is Powerful

God is love, but He is also supremely powerful.

The LORD shall go forth like a mighty man; He shall stir up [His] zeal like a man of war. He shall cry out, yes, shout aloud; He shall prevail against His enemies.
(Isaiah 42:13)

So often in our Christian walk we fail to nod to the power God commands, and lose sight of the true nature of our relationship. We are not His equal and shouldn't act as if we are. When we do, we relegate God to being as powerless as we are. Conversely, when we obey and worship as commanded He allows us to share in His power.

"If you ask anything in My name, I will do [it]."
(John 14;14)

By not knowing Him as we could, as we should, we say things like:

"I can't (fill in the blank)," when we should say: "I can."

> But Jesus looked at them and said to them, "With men this is impossible, but with God all things are possible."
> (Matthew 19:26)

This is yet another reason we have to take time and make effort to know God.

God is Jealous

God is love, but He is also jealous.

> …for you shall worship no other god, for the LORD, whose name [is] Jealous, [is] a jealous God)
> (Exodus 34:14)

A jealous God will not share you with another. If we're worshipping our career, we have a problem with God. If we're worshipping money, we have a problem with God. If we're worshipping a sports star or politician, we have a problem with God. All of these examples are forms of idolatry, putting something or someone before Him, and God will not have it. If we worship ourselves in any way, we have a problem with God.

Idolatry in any form short-circuits our relationship. God wants a one-on-one kinship with His children.

> "But you, when you pray, go into your room, and when you have shut your door, pray to your Father who [is] in the secret [place]; and your Father who sees in secret will reward you openly.
> (Matthew 6:6)

God is jealous because he is the highest, the best, so loving anything else more than Him hurts us by putting our life's priorities upside/down. His love and care for us demands that He be jealous out of love for His children.

The world puts many things of the flesh in front of us to take our eyes off of Him, but God expects us not to give in to the temptation. While we are not perfect, He expects us to try and be perfect. *For God did not call us to uncleanness, but in holiness.* (1 Thessalonians 4:7) By following His example of unquestioned righteousness, even though we will fail to be without sin (*But we are all like an unclean [thing], And all our righteousnesses [are] like filthy rags; We all fade as a leaf, And our iniquities, like the wind, Have taken us away.* Isaiah 64:6), we will have elevated God to the preeminence in our lives that He deserves and expects, as we cannot help but put Him first when we are in the process of trying to be perfect according to His standards and not our own.

God is Righteous

God is love, but He is righteous above all else.

The LORD [is] righteous in all His ways, Gracious in all His works.
(Psalm 145:17)

This is a difficult aspect of His divinity to relate to, as we cannot possibly understand a concept we cannot achieve, which brings our reason to a false perception if we depend on our own understanding. Thankfully we have the complete definition of righteous in context and application as God biblically describes righteousness from His perspective, the only perspective having relevance.

[As for] the Almighty, we cannot find Him; [He is] excellent in power, [In] judgment and abundant justice; He does not oppress.
(Job 37:23)

He shall judge the world in righteousness, And He shall administer judgment for the peoples in uprightness.
(Psalm 9:8)

He loves righteousness and justice; The earth is full of the goodness of the LORD.
(Psalm 33:5)

The LORD executes righteousness And justice for all who are oppressed.
(Psalm 103:6)

Your righteousness [is] an everlasting righteousness, And Your law [is] truth.
(Psalm 119:142)

But let him who glories glory in this, That he understands and knows Me, That I [am] the LORD, exercising loving kindness, judgment, and righteousness in the earth. For in these I delight," says the LORD.
(Jeremiah 9:24)

But, when we are not reading our Bible, not spending time in prayer, not making time to listen to Him, we are left to decipher the indecipherable with a worldly spin instead of a spiritual heart. This leads to predictable failure. When we are in fellowship and put God first in our lives, something wonderful happens. We suddenly realize that His righteousness deserves praise and devotion, if for no other reason than it is His essence, something He cares about deeply. With this understanding we are confronted with the fact that we cannot continue our worldly ways without conviction that manifests itself in required steps of repentance. If we fail to know God as He describes Himself, we delude ourselves by thinking that all is well when it is not. We rationalize that our loving God must understand we are trying the best we can, and surely that is good enough. Mistakenly, many of us are shooting for good enough instead of raising ourselves and our acts to the holy standard He commands. Sadly, we're used to lowering standards in life; that's how we improve our self-esteem even though we have fallen short of the mark; e.g., if kids can't read when they reach high school, we lower the reading requirements so failing grades become passing grades. We've done the same thing in the military, we've done it in the workplace, but I tell you the truth, God will have none of it, because He is righteous.

> I will praise the LORD according to His righteousness, And will sing praise to the name of the LORD Most High.
> (Psalm 8:17)

God is Vengeful

God is love, but He is also vengeful.

> Beloved, do not avenge yourselves, but [rather] give place to wrath; for it is written, "Vengeance [is] Mine, I will repay," says the Lord.   (Romans 12:19)

God's vengeance is used for justice and to relieve us of hate for those who have wronged us. It is an extension of His love for us, His children.

Here matters of love come full circle. At one end of the spectrum we have the only truly pure love: God's love. At the other end we have a God, who loves truth and righteousness. That requires Him to demand repayment for rebellion. This seeming dichotomy should bring your spiritual senses to attention. Think about it. God loves us so much that He sent His only Son to die in our place so we could live forever. Simply put, He allowed His Son to be treated as we should be treated, so we can be treated like His Son. There can be no greater gift. There can be no greater love. It makes sense then, that if we reject His love,

God will, because He is holy, exact an appropriate retribution commensurate with our sin. How serious a retribution?

> For if we sin willfully after we have received the knowledge of the truth, there no longer remains a sacrifice for sins, but a certain fearful expectation of judgment, and fiery indignation, which will devour the adversaries. Anyone who has rejected Moses' law dies without mercy on [the testimony of] two or three witnesses. Of how much worse punishment, do you suppose, will he be thought worthy who has trampled the Son of God underfoot, counted the blood of the covenant by which he was sanctified a common thing, and insulted the Spirit of grace? For we know Him who said, "Vengeance is Mine, I will repay," says the Lord. And again, "The LORD will judge His people." It is a fearful thing to fall into the hands of the living God. (Hebrews 10:26-31)

These are sobering verses. If we sin willfully after knowing the truth of the Word, not even the sacrifice of Jesus on the cross can pay for our sins. That, of course, is why the wages of sin is death, as without the sacrifice of Christ we cannot enter heaven. The Bible, the inspired Word of God, is saying in no uncertain terms, if we choose to continue in our sin, we were never saved in the first place, or we have subsequently exercised our free will to reject what we once embraced.

> "But the ones on the rock [are those] who, when they hear, receive the word with joy; and these have no root, who believe for a while and in time of temptation fall away. (Luke 8:13)

The sinner will then meet the same fiery fate as non-believers, who oppose the Lord.

God is Everywhere

God is love, but He is also omnipresent.

"All the way around [shall be] eighteen thousand [cubits]; and the name of the city from [that] day [shall be]: THE LORD [IS] THERE." (Ezekiel 48:35)

God is omnipresent, so the only question is: Do you live in light of the fact that God is omnipresent in your life, or do you behave as if He comes and goes according to your emotions, your present temporal circumstances? We cannot treat Him as something irrelevant to be used as necessary. Being everywhere at all times, He is to be the light of our lives, our first love. If we allow transitory conditions to overshadow His presence, in addition to keeping Him out of our heart, we risk what is often called, "dying in the winter of your faith" and not being able to right matters with the Lord prior to passing.

Where can I go from Your Spirit? Or where can I flee from Your presence? If I ascend into heaven, You [are] there; If I make my bed in hell, behold, You [are there]. [If] I take the wings of the morning, [And] dwell in the uttermost parts of the sea, Even there Your hand shall lead me, And Your right hand shall hold me. (Psalm 139:7-10)

God is there, everywhere, at all times. What a blessing to all who take joy in being His child.

God is Our Provider

God is love, but He is also our provider.

"Therefore do not worry, saying, 'What shall we eat?' or 'What shall we drink?' or 'What shall we wear?' "For after all these things the Gentiles seek. For your heavenly Father knows that you need all these things. "But seek first the kingdom of God and His righteousness, and all these things shall be added to you. (Matthew 6:31-33)

And God [is] able to make all grace abound toward you, that you, always having all sufficiency in all [things], may have an abundance for every good work.
(2 Corinthians 9:8)

And my God shall supply all your need according to His riches in glory by Christ Jesus.
(Philippians 4:19)

Every Good Thing Comes From God

It is so easy to look at what we believe we have accomplished personally while failing to give glory to the undeniable fact that everything comes from God. If you're a success in business, would you as easily be so if you were born deaf and/or blind? If you are a star athlete, would you as easily be so if you were born with no legs? Clearly, whatever we have comes from God. He is the fountainhead. Some people have more than others, but that is because God knows we can be trusted with what He provides in whatever volume.

But as God has distributed to each one, as the Lord has called each one, so let him walk. And so I ordain in all the churches.
(1 Corinthians 7:17)

From the most important details of our life to the most mundane, God is the provider. He brings male and female Christians together in marriage and gives them children to raise according to His Word. He allows bananas to grow in South America and corn to grow in Iowa so we have food to eat. He makes it rain, so we have water to drink. He gives us the forests, flowers, and other plants for beauty and oxygen to breathe. He gives us talents so we can earn a living. Whatever we need, God provides.

God is Peace

God is love, but He is also our peace.

I will give peace in the land, and you shall lie down, and none will make [you] afraid; I will rid the land of evil beasts, and the sword will not go through your land.
(Leviticus 26:6)

Man is by nature aggressive and prone to violence. It has been that way since the dawn of time as it is today. Yet we have an overall peace in His Word and in our lives because God wishes it so for His people.

Imagine what the world would be like without God's peaceful nature reigning in the earth. Every nation would be at war with every other nation. There would be total chaos in the streets of every city as the strong imposed their will on the physically weak.

Man is not peaceful by nature, but God is. It is He and He alone who keeps the delicate balance. It is only because He allows us free will that there is the existence of evil in the world, that there is war, crime, cruelty, physical abuse, killing of the unborn. Yet through it all, despite our nature of rebellion, God offers us peace. He keeps the ultimate peace in the universe so we, as His children, can live life as He provides.

The LORD will give strength to His people; The LORD will bless His people with peace.
(Psalm 29:11)

"Peace I leave with you, My peace I give to you; not as the world gives do I give to you. Let not your heart be troubled,

neither let it be afraid.
(John 14;27)

For to be carnally minded [is] death, but to be spiritually minded [is] life and peace.
(Romans 8:6)

Be anxious for nothing, but in everything by prayer and supplication, with thanksgiving, let your requests be made known to God; and the peace of God, which surpasses all understanding, will guard your hearts and minds through Christ Jesus.
(Philippians 4:6-7)

The world offers us nothing of substance. Without God it is as the old saying goes; "Life is hard, and then you die." But with the Lord we have life, peace, and life everlasting.

God is Our Judge

God is love, but he is also our judge.

He is our judge because He alone will determine whether or not we will spend eternity in heaven or hell.

I charge [you] therefore before God and the Lord Jesus Christ, who will judge the living and the dead at His appearing and His kingdom:
(2 Timothy 4:1)

He judges because we are incapable of doing so.

There is a way [that seems] right to a man, But its end [is] the way of death.
(Proverbs 14:12)

Everything we have done or ever will do will be revealed on Judgment Day. The world will know our sins, and we will receive a reward or punishment based on the obedience to, or the disobedience of, the Word of God. No one will be immune. Proving the point, the Bible tells us the judging will start with God's people.

Think about the humbling concept of being judged by our Lord. Have you ever been in traffic court? Have you ever been sued? Have you ever been a juror? If you have, you know how intimidating judges can be. They rule their courtroom with an iron fist. They can, based solely on their interpretation of the law and their real-time emotional state, send people to jail for something as simple as talking out of turn. A judge is no one to take lightly, as many people who made the mistake of doing so have found.

Imagine then how much more awesome the court of our Lord will be when we are faced with a replay of our life and how we responded to the love, grace, and mercy God freely offered. I cannot even start to picture the scene; it is too breathtaking. I only know this. God takes the fruits of our lives very seriously.

God is Our Shepherd

God is love, but He is also our shepherd who watches over and protects us.

The Lord is my shepherd; I shall not want.
(Psalm 23:1)

We have to realize that God's commandments and statutes are given for a reason. They are there to guide, not hurt us. They are there to provide us a life of abundance, not to make life difficult.

"The thief does not come except to steal, and to kill, and to

destroy. I have come that they may have life, and that they may have [it] more abundantly."
(John 10:10)

And like any good shepherd, God will try and keep us in tow so we will not be devoured by the lion (Satan) or lost to the cruel elements of the world.

Be sober, be vigilant; because your adversary the devil walks about like a roaring lion, seeking whom he may devour.
(1 Peter 5:8)

While it is in our nature to be rebellious and self-willed, thankfully, it is His nature to care for us, pick us up when we're down, heal us when we are sick, and love us even though we don't deserve it. He is the ultimate shepherd. Don't fight Him. Even if we cannot understand His ways, remember He is leading us to *green pastures* and *still waters*. He *restores* our soul. He will provide until our *cup runs over*. He will protect us so we will *fear no evil*. God is our shepherd. What He does, what He asks, what He commands, is for our own good.

God Sanctifies Us

God is love, but He is also the One who sanctifies us. He, through the sacrifice of His Son, makes us free from sin--pure enough to enter heaven.

"Speak also to the children of Israel, saying: 'Surely My Sabbaths you shall keep, for it [is] a sign between Me and you throughout your generations, that [you] may know that I [am] the LORD who sanctifies you.'"
(Exodus 31:13)

Without God we would never be free from our sin. Not now. Not ever. It is His grace that makes us productive in holiness so we may have the holy fruits of the saved. We are not sacred without His consecration, which is why we must obey His Word.

His Word is what sets us free and apart from the world.

"And you shall know the truth, and the truth shall make you free."
(John 8:32)

Without His direction we flounder. Everything we do is less than His perfection, and we flounder. When we follow the guidance of various people without deferring to God, we flounder. Without the sanctification of Christ, our names will not be written in the book of life.

And anyone not found written in the *Book of Life* was cast into the lake of fire.
(Revelation 20:15)

If God were simply the comforting force of love, as many believe, no one would ever go to hell, but we know they do. In truth, more people will go to hell than heaven. Again, this is what the Bible tells us:

"Enter by the narrow gate; for wide [is] the gate and broad [is] the way that leads to destruction, and there are many who go in by it. Because narrow [is] the gate and difficult [is] the way which leads to life, and there are few who find it."
(Matthew 7:13-14)

How can this be? How can a loving God allow more people to perish than be saved? The truth is, He doesn't. We send ourselves to hell. Our choices in life determine our fate.

"I tell you, no; but unless you repent you will all likewise perish."
(Luke 13:5)

Why is it that we refuse to acknowledge the complexity of God? Perhaps because it allows us to continue to "do our own thing" while still believing we have a claim on salvation. That's as foolish as thinking we can drive eighty-five miles-an-hour in a hospital zone without consequences. But we wouldn't do that, because we submit to the authority of the police and courts by obeying the posted speed limit.

That's also as foolish as thinking we can be late to work every day, fail to complete any assignment, and not expect to be fired. But we wouldn't do that either, as we submit to the authority of our employer by obeying the guidelines they set for performance. What a mistaken set of values we display when we correctly recognize and submit to worldly authority, yet ignore or try to find wiggle room when deciding whether or not to obey God.

> And Jesus answered and said to them, "Render to Caesar the things that are Caesar's, and to God the things that are God's." And they marveled at Him.
> (Mark 12:17)

We lust for the tinsel of life, while in many cases throwing away the pure gold of God's grace.

One Aspect of God's Character Doesn't Cancel Another

No one can answer the question of who God is beyond what the Bible allows, and even at that we can understand only a portion of what is revealed, which is why brilliant minds spend a lifetime studying the Bible and die knowing they have yet to scratch the surface.

How much more there is to God than we can possibly understand! But one thing we must know. One aspect of God's character does not cancel another. His mercy, for example, does not cancel out His righteousness. Therefore, those living in abject disobedience, while depending on God's mercy to absolve their rebellion, will be sorely disappointed.

Our permissive society has us looking for the answers to life in all the wrong places. Our spiritual disobedience has many of us feeling unhappy and unsettled. So we look to psychiatrists, psychologists, and counselors, who offer platitudes, theories, psychobabble, and drugs, but no spiritual meaning or true healing. And they, having been elevated by being asked to fix that which only God can fix, are given license to infest our hearts and minds with a worldly interpretation of God's Word. For example, society has taken the popular "love must be unconditional" mantra and woven it into the fabric of our religious beliefs. In short, we, through unmitigated arrogance, presume to tell our loving God how He should love. We want, and in some cases demand, unconditional love and mistakenly believe it relieves us of our spiritual obligation to obey.

God gives so much and asks so little in return. When we accept the sacrifice of Jesus as payment for our sins, God offers us eternal life. And still, many of us think that's not enough, that we deserve more.

Americans in particular bristle at the thought of being submissive and putting ourselves second. We have rights. No one can tell us what to do, not even God. There was once an ad campaign for an oil filter that had a car mechanic facing the camera and saying, "You can pay me now, or you can pay me later." He meant, you could buy a new filter now for a few dollars or spend hundreds of dollars later when the old filter clogs and damages the engine. The Bible says much the same thing. We can submit to God now or we can pay Him later when the cost is life everlasting.

How have we let ourselves get in the position of playing Russian roulette with our salvation? In large part it's because we have stopped putting God first in our lives.

"Nevertheless I have [this] against you, that you have left your first love."
(Revelation 2:4)

We have relegated Him to second, third, or fourth place. We take God for granted. He's there. He loves us. That's good enough. No, no it's not. It's not even close. Jesus said the greatest commandment is:

You shall love the Lord your God with all your heart, and with all your soul, and with all your mind.
(Matthew 22:37)

How can you keep faith with the greatest commandment if you don't spend time learning to know God?

For those who believe they know Him, I have to ask, do you really, or do you know a god you have created to meet your needs?

Of course, to change who God really is, one has to refine Him down to His most basic user-friendly self. Something along the lines of "God is love," period, end of story. Obviously, if this were the sum and substance of the truth, we would be free to do whatever we please without fear of judgment. But that's not Bible.

God is love, but He's so much more. And, as I said earlier, if He isn't, why worship Him? If by our actions, we have, in effect, made God our equal, why honor Him and give Him glory? If all He is to us is a supernatural copy of ourselves, He is not worthy of praise. If His Word is no more important than our opinions, He's nothing special. He's here to serve us, to answer our prayers, to meet our needs, and to ensure our salvation. We're not here to serve Him: which is why we don't go to church regularly, don't read our Bible, and don't obey, unless, of course, it suits our purpose.

Actually, many "Christians," if they are to be known by their works as the Bible describes in Matthew 7:20, must believe they are not only the equal of God, they are God's better. That's the tragic end-result of creating one's own version of God.

But, you might ask, doesn't God's mercy wipe the slate clean? Yes, God's mercy can and does make anything and everything right, and without it we would rightfully be eternally damned. But we should not presume on His mercy by continuing to use it as a license to sin. It is a mistake to assume His mercy will be received if we are in open rebellion and continued disobedience.

And his mercy [is] on them that fear him from generation to
generation.
(Luke 1:50)

When we disobey we show that we do not fear the Lord. Remember,
the majority of us will spend eternity in hell, so it is undeniable that
His mercy is not given to everyone. Who shall receive His mercy?

…but showing mercy to thousands, to those who love Me and
keep My commandments.
(Exodus 20:6)

Loving God and obeying His Word are the acts that signify the
saved. This does not deny that salvation is a gift, because it is. But obedience is the barometer of our relationship with Christ. Works will not
save you, but they tell you if you're saved.

But do you want to know, O foolish man, that faith without
works is dead?
(James 2:20)

It is impossible to overstate the importance of our obedience to the
Lord. It is central to who He is. It is the alpha and omega of sin, for it
is Him we sin against.

For as by one man's disobedience many were made sinners, so
also by one Man's obedience many will be made righteous.
(Romans 5:19)

Paul brings into focus the importance of obedience when he wrote:

…casting down arguments and every high thing that exalts itself against the knowledge of God, bringing every thought into
captivity to the obedience of Christ. That is our charge, bringing

every thought into captivity to the obedience of Christ.
(II Corinthians 10:5)

Is God first in your life? Does your life give Him praise? Luke 1:50 and Exodus 20:6 are quintessential examples of the cause-and-effect displayed in God's Word. To be able to understand the Bible, our blueprint for life, you have to know the author. You have to know God as He describes Himself, and the more you learn of Him the more you realize He has a multi-faceted view of how we are to be saved. It is not simply:

…that if you confess with your mouth the Lord Jesus and believe in your heart that God has raised Him from the dead, you will be saved.
(Romans 10:9)

Nor is it just John 3:16. Such simplification is contextually myopic. Salvation is not a one-dimensional stand-alone view of the many building blocks that lead to spending eternity in God's presence.

However, just like describing God in one sentence, our want-it-now, limited-attention-span society has distilled salvation down to what can be accomplished in a few minutes at any given altar call. We like that version of salvation. It's quick, painless, and offers a lifetime guarantee regardless of our fruits. This is not to say one cannot be saved at a singular altar call, because such things can and do happen—often. But just as often, if not more so, an altar call is absent the heart-felt substance and personal commitment that would reflect true acceptance of the gift.

One of my father's favorite sayings was, "Sometimes something is so simple that it's hard." Think about that, and then apply it to the question posed as this chapter's heading: Who is God? The truth is, everyone should be able to answer the question because it's like an open-book quiz. The answer is right there in front of you. How much simpler can it be? Pick up your Bible!

Now ask yourself, why are Satan and his false teachers trying to make the answer even simpler? There must be a reason. And, knowing the Satan God describes in His book, his motivation must be sinister. He comes to kill and steal and destroy.

Here's a possible answer we must consider. Satan knows we're spiritually lazy, and he knows we like to do what we want when we want, so he distills God's own description of Himself, so we will believe our disobedience has no consequences. If God is love, and only love, we have nothing to fear in our rebellion.

But if God, who only tells the truth, is who He says He is, we had better get with the spiritual program, now!

Nominal Christians are like wife abusers who, after beating their spouses, then hold them and say how much they love them….until the next beating. We can't say we love the Lord, abuse His Word, and then expect to be believed, much less reap the reward of a heavenly destination when our time on earth is done. No, we will reap the harvest we have planted, and most of us know that.

While not willing to accept our fate; i.e., we know what we deserve, but being the arrogant creatures we are, we're not about to accept it without a fight.

What follows is a play on the proverb, "If the mountain won't come to Mahomet, Mahomet must go to the mountain." If things aren't as we wish them, we have to make adjustments. In this case it means if God won't be moved (changed), He must be destroyed, for if He is destroyed, we no longer are disobedient and living in rebellion.

A secular analogy: America has a political rebellion that destroys all order. While the laws of the land may still be on the books, without police, courts, and government at the local, state, and national level, all laws are rendered moot.

Knowing God as He describes Himself is not just a spiritual exercise; it is crucial for directing our efforts regarding eternity. But if we don't truly know God, it is illogical to fear him.

And they were all amazed, and they glorified God and were
filled with fear, saying, "We have seen strange things today!"
(Luke 5:26)

The gestalt here is, by diminishing God we believe, incorrectly so,
that we have little to fear in our willful rebellion.

The more we diminish God, the less we stand in awe of Him. This
eventually leads to apostasy, a critical-mass point. In apostasy, many
view God as an impediment to their wants and needs. Without God
being their guardrail, their lives will eventually carom into the pit of
secularism.

The real One true God cannot, will not, be ignored. Society's version of God is of no importance. He is love, nothing more. For us to
live in disobedience, He must be brought to His knees to worship at
the altar of a greater god—man.

Obviously, based on the decline of our civilization, most people
don't want to know God, except on their own terms. One path leads to
destruction; one leads to streets paved with gold.

"Enter by the narrow gate; for wide [is] the gate and broad [is]
the way that leads to destruction, and there are many who go
in by it. Because narrow [is] the gate and difficult [is] the way
which leads to life, and there are few who find it."
(Matthew 7:13-14)

Out of rebellion, societies throughout history have chosen the former at the expense of the latter. Sodom and Gomorrah, Rome, Egypt,
Germany, Japan, Russia, Cuba, and others. History is replete with civi-
lizations, who in their own way sought to destroy the Lord. Again, it is
the principle that those who will not learn from history are doomed to
repeat it. But the false allure of being our own god is powerful beyond
mere words.

Throughout time there have been people who had to be destroyed
for society to have its way. People of character who stood for the truth

no matter the consequences, up to and including death. For men of honor, there are things worse than death. To the secular, death is the 800-pound gorilla in the room. What we fear is often a telltale sign of what we do or do not believe in.

God's righteousness brings conviction, and that gets in the way of us doing our own thing, and we live in a time when that will not be tolerated. Everything we do wrong is always someone else's fault. How dare God suggest otherwise!

Society says that if it feels good, do it. It is not concerned with consequences. But there are consequences, so, since we won't bend our arrogant knees to a higher authority, we'll have to remove the author of said consequences - God.

God must be removed from our consciousness, not because He's weak, but because He's all-powerful, and as such gets in our way. He's like a sore that won't heal. He's always there to convict us in the hope that we will turn to Him with love and respect. But too often our hypocrisy gets in the way of true discipleship - witness 9/11. Prior to that, America as a society did everything it could to kick God out of our lives, institutions, and government(s) Immediately after 9/11 our hedonistic leaders called for a National Day of Prayer. And now, with little passage of time, we are right back to removing God from our lives.

We can try and diminish His power all we want, but before we do we should at least know what we're up against.

The following is taken from *The Attributes of God* by A.W. Pink (first printing-1930),

(http://www.pbministries.org/books/pink/Attributes/attrib_09.htm).

"We cannot have a right conception of God unless we think of Him as all-powerful, as well as all-wise. He who cannot do what he will and perform all his pleasure cannot be God. As God hath a will to resolve what He deems good, so has He power to execute His will.

The power of God is that ability and strength whereby He can bring to pass whatsoever He pleases, whatsoever His infinite wisdom may direct, and whatsoever the infinite purity of His will may resolve.

. . . As holiness is the beauty of all God's attributes, so power is that which gives life and action to all the perfections of the Divine nature. How vain would be the eternal counsels, if power did not step in to execute them. Without power His mercy would be but feeble pity, His promises an empty sound, His threatenings a mere scarecrow. God's power is like Himself: infinite, eternal, incomprehensible; it can neither be checked, restrained, nor frustrated by the creature. (S. Charnock).

"God hath spoken once; twice have I heard this, that power belongeth unto God" (Ps. 62:11) "God hath spoken once": nothing more is necessary! Heaven and earth shall pass away, but His word abideth forever. God hath spoken once: how befitting His Divine majesty! We poor mortals may speak often and yet fail to be heard. He speaks but once and the thunder of His power is heard on a thousand hills. "The Lord also thundered in the heavens, and the Highest gave His voice; hailstones and coals of fire. Yea, He sent out His arrows, and scattered them; and He shot out lightnings, and discomfited them. Then the channels of waters were seen and the foundations of the world were discovered at Thy rebuke, O Lord, at the blast of the breath of Thy nostrils" (Ps. 18:13-15).

"God hath spoken once": behold His unchanging authority. "For who in the heaven can be compared unto the Lord? who among the sons of the mighty can be likened unto the Lord?" (Ps. 89:6) "And all the inhabitants of the earth are reputed as nothing: and He doeth according to His will in the army of heaven, and among the inhabitants of the earth: and none can stay His hand, or say unto Him, What dost Thou?" (Dan. 4:35) This was openly displayed when God became incarnate and tabernacled among men. To the leper He said, "I Will, be thou clean, and immediately his leprosy was cleansed" (Matt. 8:3) To one who had lain in the grave four days He cried, "Lazarus, come forth," and the dead came forth. The stormy wind and the angry wave were hushed at a single word from Him. A legion of demons could not resist His authoritative command.

"Power belongeth unto God," and to Him alone. Not a creature in the entire universe has an atom of power save what God delegates. But

God's power is not acquired, nor does it depend upon any recognition by any other authority. It belongs to Him inherently.

God's power is like Himself, self-existent, self-sustained. The mightiest of men cannot add so much as a shadow of increased power to the Omnipotent One. He sits on no buttressed throne and leans on no assisting arm. His court is not maintained by His courtiers, nor does it borrow its splendor from His creatures. He is Himself the great central source and Originator of all power (C. H. Spurgeon).

Not only does all creation bear witness to the great power of God, but also to His entire independency of all created things. Listen to His own challenge: "Where wast thou when I laid the foundations of the earth? declare, if thou hast understanding. Who hath laid the measures thereof, if thou knowest? or who hath stretched the line upon it? Whereupon are the foundations thereof fastened or who laid the cornerstone thereof?" (Job 38:4-6) How completely is the pride of man laid in the dust!

Power is also used as a name of God, the Son of man sitting at the right hand of power (Mark 14:62), that is, at the right hand of God. God and power are so inseparable that they are reciprocated. As His essence is immense, not to be confined in place; as it is eternal, not to be measured in time; so it is almighty, not to be limited in regard of action (S. Charnock).

"Lo, these are parts of His ways:" but how little a portion is heard of Him? but the thunder of His power who can understand? (Job 26:14) Who is able to count all the monuments of His power? Even that which is displayed of His might in the visible creation is utterly beyond our powers of comprehension, still less are we able to conceive of omnipotence itself. There is infinitely more power lodged in the nature of God than is expressed in all His works.

"Parts of His ways" we behold in creation, providence, redemption, but only a "little part" of His might is seen in them. Remarkably is this brought out in Habakkuk 3:4: "and there was the hiding of His power." It is scarcely possible to imagine anything more grandiloquent than the imagery of this whole chapter, yet nothing in it surpasses the nobility of this statement. The prophet (in vision) beheld the mighty God scattering the hills and overturning the mountains, which one would think afforded an amazing demonstration of His power Nay, says our verse, that is rather the "hiding" than the displaying of His power. What is meant? This: so inconceivable, so immense, so uncontrollable is the power of Deity, that the fearful convulsions which He works in nature conceal more than they reveal of His infinite might!

It is very beautiful to link together the following passages: "He walketh upon the waves of the sea" (Job 9:8), which expresses God's uncontrollable power. "He walketh in the circuit of Heaven" (Job 22:14), which tells of the immensity of His presence. "He walketh upon the wings of the wind" (Ps. 104:3), which signifies the amazing swiftness of His operations. This last expression is very remarkable. It is not that "He flieth," or "runneth," but that He "walketh" and that, on the very "wings of the wind"—on the most impetuous of the elements, tossed into utmost rage, and sweeping along with almost inconceivable rapidity, yet they are under His feet, beneath His perfect control!

Let us now consider God's power in creation. "The heavens are Thine, the earth also is Thine, as for the world and the fulness thereof, Thou hast founded them. The north and the south Thou hast created them" (Ps. 89:11, 12) Before man can work be must have both tools and materials, but God began with nothing, and by His word alone out of nothing made all things. The intellect cannot grasp it. God "spake and it was done, He commanded and it stood fast" (Ps. 33:9) Primeval matter heard His voice. "God said, Let there be. . .and it was so" (Gen. 1) Well may we exclaim, "Thou hast a mighty arm: strong is Thy hand, high is Thy right hand" (Ps. 89:13).

Who, that looks upward to the midnight sky; and, with an eye of reason, beholds its rolling wonders; who can forbear inquiring, Of what were their mighty orbs formed? Amazing to relate, they were produced without materials. They sprung from emptiness itself. The stately fabric of universal nature emerged out of nothing. What instruments were used by the Supreme Architect to fashion the parts with such exquisite niceness, and give so beautiful a polish to the whole?

How was it all connected into one finely-proportioned and nobly finished structure? A bare fiat accomplished all. Let them be, said God. He added no more; and at once the marvelous edifice arose, adorned with every beauty, displaying innumerable perfections, and declaring amidst enraptured seraphs its great Creator's praise. "By the word of the Lord were the heavens made, and all the host of them by the breath of His mouth," Psa. 150:1 (James Hervey, 1789).

Consider God's power in preservation. No creature has power to preserve itself. "Can the rush grow up without mire? can the flag grow up without water?" (Job 8:11) Both man and beast would perish if there were not herbs for food, and herbs would wither and die if the earth were not refreshed with fruitful showers. Therefore is God called the Preserver of "man and beast" (Ps. 36:6) "He upholdeth all things by the word of His power" (Heb 1:3) What a marvel of Divine power is the prenatal life of every human being! That an infant can live at all, and for so many months, in such cramped and filthy quarters, and that without breathing, is unaccountable without the power of God. Truly He "holdeth our soul in life" (Ps. 66:9).

The preservation of the earth from the violence of the sea is another plain instance of God's might. How is that raging element kept pent within those limits wherein He first lodged it, continuing its channel, without overflowing the earth and dashing in pieces the lower part of the creation? The natural situation of the water is to be above the earth, because it is lighter, and to be immediately under the air, because it is heavier. Who restrains the natural quality of it? certainly man does not, and cannot. It is the fiat of its Creator which alone bridles it: And said, "Hitherto shalt thou come, but no further: and here shall thy proud waves be stayed" (Job 38:11) What a standing monument of the power of God is the preservation of the world!

Consider God's power in government. Take His restraining the malice of Satan. "The devil, as a roaring lion, walketh about, seeking whom he may devour" (1 Pet. 5:8) He is filled with hatred against God, and with fiendish enmity against men, particularly the saints. He that envied Adam in paradise, envies us the pleasure of enjoying any of God's blessings. Could he have his will, he would treat all the same way he treated Job: he would send fire from heaven on the fruits of the earth, destroying the cattle, cause a wind to overthrow our houses, and cover our bodies with boils. But, little as men may realize it, God bridles him to a large extent, prevents him from carrying out his evil designs, and confines him within His ordinations.

So too God restrains the natural corruption of men. He suffers sufficient outbreakings of sin to show what fearful havoc has been wrought by man's apostasy from his Maker, but who can conceive the frightful lengths to which men would go were God to remove His curbing hand? "Their mouth is full of cursing and bitterness their feet are swift to shed blood" (Rom. 3) This is the nature of every descendant of Adam. Then what unbridled licentiousness and headstrong folly would triumph in the world, if the power of God did not interpose to lock down the floodgates of it! See Psalm 93:3,4.

Consider God's power in judgment. When He smites, none can resist Him: see Ezekiel 22:14. How terribly this was exemplified at the Flood! God opened the windows of heaven and broke up the great fountains of the deep, and (excepting those in the ark) the entire human race, helpless before the storm of His wrath, was swept away. A shower of fire and brimstone from heaven, and the cities of the plain were exterminated. Pharaoh and all his hosts were impotent when God blew upon them at the Red Sea. What a terrific word is that in Romans 9:22: "What if God, willing to show wrath, and to make His power known, endured with much long-suffering the vessels of wrath fitted to destruction." God is going to display His mighty power upon the reprobate not merely by incarcerating them in Gehenna, but by supernaturally preserving their bodies as well as souls amid the eternal burnings of the Lake of Fire.

Well may all tremble before such a God! To treat with impunity One who can crush us more easily than we can a moth, is a suicidal policy. To openly defy Him who is clothed with omnipotence, who can rend us in pieces or cast into Hell any moment He pleases, is the very height of insanity. To put it on its lowest ground, it is but the part of wisdom to heed His command, "Kiss the Son. lest He be angry, and ye perish from the way, when His wrath is kindled but a little" (Ps. 2:12).

Well may the enlightened soul adore such a God! The wondrous and infinite perfections of such a Being call for fervent worship. If men of might and renown claim the admiration of the world, how much more should the power of the Almighty fill us with wonderment and homage. "Who is like unto Thee, O Lord, among the who is like Thee, glorious in holiness, fearful in praises, doing wonders?" (Ex. 15:11).

Well may the saint trust such a God! He is worthy of implicit confidence. Nothing is too hard for Him. If God were stinted in might and had a limit to His strength we might well despair. But seeing that He is clothed with omnipotence, no prayer is too hard for Him to answer, no need too great for Him to supply, no passion too strong for Him to subdue; no temptation too powerful for Him to deliver from, no misery too deep for Him to relieve. "The Lord is the strength of my life; of whom shall I be afraid?" (Ps. 27:1) "Now unto Him that is able to do exceeding abundantly above all that we ask or think, according to the power that worketh in us, unto Him be glory in the church by Christ Jesus throughout all ages, world without end. Amen" (Eph. 3:20,21) (Arthur W. Pink 1886-1952)

Don't be concerned that this was written so long ago, because it's as accurate today as it was then, as God and His Word never change.

The point is, the wonderful loving might of the Lord is the very reason He must be wiped from our consciousness. He is an impediment to everything modern society stands for. But while we are applauding our pathetic "accomplishments," we'd better be aware that we've declared war on a power we cannot even begin to comprehend. The inequality of the battle will not stop us, such is the arrogance of man, but when the dust settles we need to know that "It is a fearful thing to fall into the hands of the living God." (Hebrews 10:31)

They Don't Want to Know God

Politics makes strange bedfellows; so does religion, as often the objectives of those with seemingly differing point of views dovetail, or, at the least, become symbiotic. God's enemies, those who overtly want to destroy Him, are the followers of Satan (evil) *and* nominal Christians. Evil wants God gone because He and He alone stands between it and world domination (a hell on earth scenario) Nominal Christians, those Christians exposed as pretenders by their rebellious disobedience, want God covertly destroyed, because He gets in the way of their self-directed lives.

The sad truth is, too often evil knows the real God, while we don't.

Evil knows God, because it knows the importance of knowing its enemy.

Nominal Christians don't, because they don't want to know.

2

WHY GOD MUST BE KILLED

When thinking about killing God (something I pray you don't contemplate) we have to ask ourselves, why? Why would we want to eradicate an entity so powerful and loving?

Therein lies the answer to the question; God is too lovingly powerful for Him to co-exist with our selfish society. A society that has come to believe that man is God, and that we cannot co-exist with another God who sees Himself as more powerful than we are.

For if He's God, then we're not. And if we're not, our decadent lifestyle and moral decline cannot be justified under the guise of tolerance and enlightenment.

No, instead, (following the Bible guidelines) we are wretched souls, who are supervising our own demise.

Have you ever noticed that each society that has fallen throughout history has a period right before its falling that can correctly be termed anarchy?

Anarchy:

- An absence of government
- A state of lawlessness or political disorder due to the absence of governmental authority
- A <u>utopian</u> (my emphasis) society of individuals, who enjoy complete freedom without government
- Absence or denial of any authority or established order (source: Merriam-Webster.com)

Now apply that definition to the character of America. An honest appraisal will lead you to an inescapable conclusion; America is rapidly escalating into an advanced form of anarchy. It's not apparent at first because we're in a period of declining freedoms, which makes one wonder if we are absent government authority.

Truth is, government has never been more oppressive here at home as it is now. We can barely take a breath without having to ask government, at the local, state, and national level, for permission.

No, lack of government intrusion in our lives is not the problem. Quite the contrary. While not comparing our government to the pre-WWII government of Germany, there is a principle comparison that deserves attention.

First they came for the <u>communists</u>, and I didn't speak out because I wasn't a communist.

Then they came for the <u>socialists</u>, and I didn't speak out because I wasn't a socialist.

Then they came for the <u>trade unionists</u>, and I didn't speak out because I wasn't a trade unionist.

Then they came for the <u>Jews</u>, and I didn't speak out because I wasn't a Jew.

Then they came for the <u>Catholics</u>, and I didn't speak out because I wasn't a Catholic.

Then they came for me, and there was no one left to speak for me. (Pastor Martin Niemöller (1892–1984)

In America today everyone looks to government to solve our problems, when the truth is Ronald Reagan was right, "Government does not solve problems; it subsidizes them." Seriously, sit down and write down all the problems our government solves. Except for the defense of our nation by our heroic military, all government does is make our lives more difficult or destroy our God-given right of free will. We are like the German elite described by Pastor Niemöller, except in our case we're not talking about groups of people per se, but our freedoms. We sit quietly in our self-righteousness, because this or that right doesn't pertain to us directly, and soon we will wake up and find that our rights, too, have been taken, and there's no one to help us.

The Congress, Executive branch, and our courts have all been corrupted and are now part of the problem, when we so desperately need solutions.

Here's another historical truth—for a government to exercise complete control over the governed, religion must be abolished, as they are like oil and water.

Do not be unequally yoked together with unbelievers. For what fellowship has righteousness with lawlessness? And what communion has light with darkness?
(2 Corinthians 6:14)

It's a law of nature that light and darkness cannot inhabit the same space at the same time. So, since government's objectives differ from God's, one has to go. Society says God is the loser to the ascension of man. This is not theory; it's history. Examples include: Rome, Germany, Japan, U.S.S.R., China, and Cuba. There are lesser examples, but the point should be made. As any government gets stronger, the church must be diminished and eventually destroyed. They cannot exist together.

This take doesn't have to be, but it always has been because man continually fails to heed the admonition: "Absolute power corrupts absolutely." The rebuke arose as part of a quotation of *John Emerich Edward Dalberg Acton, first Baron Acton* (1834–1902) The historian and moralist, who was otherwise known simply as Lord Acton, expressed this opinion in a letter to Bishop Mandell Creighton in 1887: "Power tends to corrupt, and absolute power corrupts absolutely. Great men are almost always bad men."

Think of the power of our government, and then think of those running it. It is beyond scary that our government has degenerated into the freedom-killer it has become. The power of the government, at all levels, can be directly tied to the demise of the holy church, run by men who long-ago ditched the Gospel for a go-along-to-get-along doctrine.

This doctrine has given birth to churches embracing the homosexual lifestyle, marching for a woman's right to an abortion, the destruction of our national sovereignty, and the destruction of a parent's right to raise their children as they and God see fit. And the list goes on.

In too large a part it is the fault of the church hierarchy that we are in the fix we're in today. Like the Germans in pre-WWII Germany, clergy remained silent thinking they could make a deal with the devil known as government. They ignored the warning from Sir Edmund Burke, "All that is necessary for the triumph of evil is that good men do nothing."

Ask yourself this; do you believe the men who penned and signed our Constitution would be party to the mess now in Washington? Would they go along to get along? Would they erode our freedom to increase their personal power and wealth? Ask yourself this; why are virtually all members of Congress multi-millionaires, even though they may at first have come to Washington with little or no wealth? The point is, our system of government is so systemically flawed now that it now controls the lives of those governed, with or without their consent. We revolted against the King of England for far less than the Washington royalty does against us each and every day.

The ruling elite among us have worked for decades to remove God from our government, courts, education system, family life, workplace, and every other important aspect of our lives. And then what does it do when we experience a 9/11? It calls for a day of prayer.

Hypocrisy?

Not really. Rather it's a form of control.

It shifts responsibility of bad news from government to God. You're heard the atheistically pious lament, "How can a loving God let this happen?" Our government will use and abuse God as they see fit, but it is fooling no one except those who refuse to see.

Even so you also outwardly appear righteous to men, but inside
you are full of hypocrisy and lawlessness.
(Matthew 23:28)

To make this point I offer a few examples to ensure you can see
why our society can no longer exist with God. Why He must be killed.

Abortion

In 1973 the Supreme Court decided 7-2 that a woman had a right
to abort (i.e., kill) her unborn child. The basis of their finding was
found in the 14th Amendment under the right to privacy. History has
proven (by going through the papers of the then justices) without
doubt that the ruling was decided first, and justified later. Point being,
this was not a constitutional finding, but a political one.

The rights of women were at the forefront of the Progressive movement, and the court was not about to challenge half the population.
It found instead that its best interest was served by acquiescing to the
wants of the many.

Worse yet, the law was able to morph into something we were
promised would never happen: abortion on demand. The law was so
poorly constructed that such abomination was able to occur right in
front of our eyes. Nothing was done to stop it.

The original case was a rape case, where we were made to feel sorry
for the victim, thereby confusing the two issues to the advantage of
the radical feminists who pushed the matter. Surely, they argued, a
rape victim shouldn't be made to carry a child to term; surely she has
suffered enough. Little thought was given to the suffering of the child,
who was to be aborted (the baby was born before the case was decided).

Decades later we found out an important fact: while the case itself
does not mention rape per se, the "rape angle" was used repeatedly in
the Progressive's public-relations efforts, which subsequently affected
the mindset of the court. The important point being: the case was a
fraud from day one. Norma McCorvey (Jane Roe) later in life admitted

there had been no rape.

Of course, the Supreme Court had no right to rule on the matter, because abortion is not mentioned in the Constitution, which is why it should have been sent back to the states for adjudication where it rightfully belonged.

As those on the Right knew at the time, a woman's right to an abortion would expand each and every year, which is exactly what happened. That's why we went from the right to an abortion, at first based on the trimester doctrine, to the "viability" of the child, to abortion on demand, which led to abortion clinics like the offices of Dr. Kermit Gosnell in Pennsylvania. What has been done in too many clinics like Dr. Gosnell's makes the experiments of Dr. Josef Mengele, the Nazi "doctor" who experimented on pregnant women and innocent children, look like nothing to be concerned with.

In some abortion clinics, children are born alive and left to die or are killed outright by severing their spine. In some cases, in order to comply with the law, the child is dismembered in the mother's womb, so it can be said that the child was not born, so technically it wasn't killed.

Many pro-abortion people use the term *fetus* instead of *baby* or *child*, but that's using semantics to obscure the horrible truth that a child is being killed.

And if it's not a living thing, as Progressives claim, killing it is not necessary.

The pro-abortion crowd knows the truth of their crime against humanity, which is why they immediately run to an acquiescing court the moment the pro-life movement tries to run ads on television showing the results of an abortion. The courts, to date, have always found in the favor of the pro-abortion position, usually claiming that the pictures and videos of an abortion are too upsetting graphically to be shown in a venue that can be seen by innocent children. Ironic, huh. The pro-abortion people want to save their children the trauma of seeing those very people kill a child they don't want born.

Politicians, not wanting to offend half the voting population, usually go along with the pro-abortion Progressives. They say Roe v. Wade is the law of the land, and there's nothing they can do. Question: Wasn't slavery the law of the land until America finally decided to step up and do the right thing? Hiding behind existing law, especially laws that are clearly wrong, is just that—hiding. America so desperately needs leaders who will do the right thing for the right reason, but today we have politicians, not leaders.

Satan, the father of all lies and the master of incrementalism, knows that people will not jump from A to Z. Rather they must be taken from A to Z one step at a time. For example, if America knew that Roe v. Wade would lead to Dr. Kermit Gosnell, Roe v. Wade never would have been decided as it was. If we had known in 1970 that legalizing abortion for rape, incest and the health of the mother would lead to abortion-on-demand in 2013, abortion would have never been legalized. Or if it were, the parameters would have been specifically narrow.

It is inherent in a woman that she want to love and protect her children. Therefore, the idea of legalized abortion should alarm us as a society. Even most animal species will die to protect their own. Yet in less than five decades many woman have been "refined" to feel that their children are too often a bother that needs to be destroyed so they can get on with their lives.

Even the 1970s Supreme Court did not intend for abortion to be a form of birth control, which it now is. How could we, as a society, have allowed our love of innocent children, who are unable to defend themselves, to be legislated out of us? The answer is simple: we no longer worship God and all He stands for; we worship self.

The Progressive Left, when pushing for more and more welfare to keep a large voting block in its financial-slavery control, will often say, "Any society, any nation, is judged on the basis of how it treats its weakest members; the last, the least, the littlest" (Pope John Paul II) But they will ignore that very same quote as it applies to children yet born. Who's weaker than an unborn child? Who's the least, the littlest? A mother has a lot of rights before becoming pregnant, but making someone else pay for her errors should not be one of them.

As for rape and incest, the case for the "unassailable" right to an abortion, they only make up less than two % of pregnancies. That's not to make light of the problem, but it does make the case that we shouldn't make public policy that affects millions of people based on the unfortunate circumstances of a few.

Contrary to prevailing belief, those against abortion are totally dedicated to helping victims of rape and incest by providing care and medical expenses to save the life of the child. Adoption services are provided should the mother decide it appropriate. This is a truth almost never reported by our Left-leaning media.

How many abortions have occurred
since the 1973 decision in Roe v. Wade?

According to the Alan Gutmacher Institute, a proponent of abortion-on-demand, the number exceeds fifty million. If you do the yearly math, that number seems "small," but I use it here, as hopefully their political bent will head-off any argument, as whatever the number, it's too big if it's more than one. I hope even pro-abortionists would be horrified to realize that America has killed so many of its children. That's more children than the population of each individual state in the Union. It's twelve million more children than the population of California, our largest state. If you start with the state with the lowest population (WY) and work your way up, we've aborted a number of children equal to the entire population of twenty-seven of our states combined. As a percentage of present-day population, fifty million is equal to sixteen % of our 313 million citizens.

Think about our reaction if the population of 27 of our states had been destroyed by an outside force since 1973!

America, through deception of those inspired by Satan, has become hypocritically double-minded. For example, we have passed a myriad of laws regarding smoking, in no small part because of the potential of secondhand smoke harming innocent children. It is estimated by the Center for Disease Control that approximate 2,000 deaths a year are caused by secondhand smoke, and the number of children's deaths is only a small percentage of that. The argument has always been, "If we can save the life of one child, it's worth it." The way I feel about children, I don't wish to argue that sentiment. That said, I do want to bring to your attention the gross and blatant hypocrisy of a policy that says a mother has no right to smoke around her kids because she *might* harm them, but does have the right to kill them in her womb, or, sadly now, outside her womb as they are born.

Just how bad are things?

Perhaps a story printed on 8 July, 2013, written by J. Matt Barber under the title *Hail Satan!* will help you understand. "The New Pro-Choice Mantra" says it best: "In the war between life and death, all eyes are on Texas as the Lone Star State legislature is poised to pass a sweeping late-term abortion ban. Gov. Rick Perry has pledged to sign the bill into law. The lines have been clearly drawn surrounding this progress toward equality and civil rights for pre-born Americans. Not surprisingly, as the pro-abortion side loses legislative battle after legislative battle, its "true colors" are coming into focus. Those colors are darker than many might have imagined."

I continue here, paraphrasing Barber's article: During all civil-rights struggles there occurs, it seems, a flashpoint in time that indelibly sears into the conscience of a culture, with clarity, the profound realization that one side represents good and the other side evil. Who can forget the images in the 1960s of law- enforcement officials turning the hoses – and the dogs – on peaceful African-America demonstrators for merely petitioning their government for racial equality? Millions of fence-sitters across America witnessed this gross injustice on television, sat up in their chairs and finally said: "This is wrong. I will not stand for it."

Although, our pro-abortion media will not likely give it much coverage, a similar flashpoint of clarity occurred this past Tuesday in the Texas State House as pro-abortion activists, throughout the day, shouted "Hail Satan!" in an effort to drown out pro-life speeches and an impromptu rendering of "Amazing Grace." CNN's Josh Rubin confirmed this astonishing display by tweeting on site: "Crowd of anti-abortion activists giving speeches while a group of people chant 'hail Satan' in the background."

I would like to take a moment to pause and personally thank our Satan-hailing friends for their brutally wicked honesty. What may have seemed, at the time, a glib bid to mock the peaceful Christians in attendance has, instead, demonstrated to the world exactly from whom (or what) derives the revolting inhumanity that is all things "pro-choice."

Understandably, many now complain that this frank display of "pro-choice" allegiance to the prince of darkness has hurt the multi-billion dollar baby-killing biz. They're right. It has. It's blown away the smokescreen of euphemistic "pro-choice" rhetoric and propaganda to expose-naked beneath, that which lies at abortion's inglorious core: death, death and more death.

Indeed, the very Satan they hail was the first "pro-choicer." While Jesus is "the Way, the Truth and the Life," Satan is the end, the lie and death itself. While Christ is the "author of life," Satan is the author of abortion. Our "pro-choice" friends in Texas have now revealed that they at least intuitively recognize this reality.

> "For the mouth speaks what the heart is full of. A good man brings good things out of the good stored up in him, and an evil man brings evil things out of the evil stored up in him. But I tell you that everyone will have to give account on the Day of Judgment for every empty word they have spoken. For by your words you will be acquitted, and by your words you will be condemned."
> (Matthew 12:34-37)

Do you consider yourself "pro-choice?" Perhaps it's time to reconsider. When "pro-choicers" find themselves shouting "hail Satan!" over a chorus of "Amazing Grace" at a gathering geared toward saving babies, maybe it's time to dust off that ol' worldview and give it a second look.

Scripture warns:

"The coming of the lawless one will be in accordance with how Satan works. He will use all sorts of displays of power through signs and wonders that serve the lie, and all the ways that wickedness deceives those who are perishing. They perish because they refused to love the truth and so be saved. For this reason God sends them a powerful delusion so that they will believe the lie and so that all will be condemned who have not believed the truth but have delighted in wickedness."
(2 Thessalonians 2:10-12)

If you answer to "pro-choice," you're only deceiving yourself, my friend. You're "delighting in wickedness." Pro-choice to do what? Pro-choice to dismember alive a baby girl in her mother's womb. That's wicked. That's evil – objective, absolute evil – every time and without exception.

That's abortion.

Abortion is death. If you're "pro-choice," you're pro-abortion and, consequently, pro-death. As the babies you should be protecting perish, so, too, do you perish. You are perishing in the spirit, which is a fate worse than physical death. It's forever.

The precious aborted babies you refuse to defend – the babies you condemn to death – will see God. Ultimately, they will have eternal life. But because you "refuse to love the truth" and "delight in wickedness," Scripture warns that, unless you repent and are saved, you will not see God. If you believe that this is about "women's reproductive rights," then you're laboring "under a powerful delusion." You "serve the lie."

Whether you know it or not, you serve Satan.

Open your eyes.

As goes the refrain, "I once was lost, but now I'm found, was blind, but now I see." You can still be found. You can still see. A big step in the right direction is first admit this painful truth: "Pro-choice" is pro-death.

Join the right side of history. Join the side of good over evil. Join the side of life over death.

Be pro-life."

Barber's article is worth study as it strips away any sociological veneer that tries to hide what abortion really is--the same thought process that calls abortion a "choice." A woman's right to choose is so much more palatable than the word abortion, but it doesn't change the truth. And when you have a group believing that's it is permissible, even preferred, to terminate a living person, rather than be responsible for their own actions, chanting "Hail, Satan!" while others believing in life are singing Amazing Grace, well, perhaps it's time to sit down and perform a spiritual gut check.

And what does God say about abortion?

First we have to put away the notion that a "fetus" is nothing more than a mass of goo not worthy of concern.

> "All that open the womb [are] Mine, and every male firstborn among your livestock, [whether] ox or sheep.
> (Exodus 34:19)

> Did not He who made me in the womb make them? Did not the same One fashion us in the womb?
> (Job 31:15)

> Behold, children [are] a heritage from the LORD, The fruit of the womb [is] a reward.
> (Psalms 127:3)

> For You formed my inward parts; You covered me in my mother's womb.
> (Psalms 139:13)

Thus says the LORD who made you And formed you from the womb, [who] will help you: 'Fear not, O Jacob My servant; And you, Jeshurun, whom I have chosen.
(Isaiah 44:2)

"Before I formed you in the womb I knew you; Before you were born I sanctified you; I ordained you a prophet to the nations."
(Jeremiah 1:5)

But when it pleased God, who separated me from my mother's womb and called [me] through His grace.
(Galatians 1:15)

Lastly, we have the commandment not to kill.

You have heard that it was said to those of old, 'You shall not murder, and whoever murders will be in danger of the judgment.'
(Matthew 5:21)

One of the tools of evil is to call evil good and good evil. This is a case in point. Abortionists will say that an abortion is not murder, not killing. But it is, by definition, exactly that. If "something" living is not being destroyed, killed, then an abortion is not necessary. It's akin to the defense argument in the Kermit Gosnell murder/abortion case. If the fully formed babies were already dead, why was it necessary to sever their spinal cords? With a "standard" abortion the same holds true; if something alive is not being killed, the abortion is not necessary. How perverse we've become.

Be honest: which view reveals goodness? God's view, or those who abort children.

I have said for decades now that when the history of America is written, 1973, the year of Roe v. Wade, will be designated the year that America turned its back on good and embraced evil.

Woe to those who call evil good, and good evil; Who put darkness for light, and light for darkness; Who put bitter for sweet, and sweet for bitter! Woe to [those who are] wise in their own eyes, And prudent in their own sight!
(Isaiah 5:20-21)

We are reaping our "reward."

Homosexuality

Let's visit another example to make the point that God must die. The subject is homosexuality.

The American Psychiatric Association removed homosexuality as a mental disorder from the APA's *Diagnostic and Statistical Manual Of Mental Disorders* (DSM-II) in 1973. Interesting that it was the same year as the passage of Roe v. Wade. The APA ruling that changed hundreds of years of psychiatric precedent throughout the world, was a capitulation to the very aggressive homosexual lobby, and gave the heretofore deviant behavior (as described by the previous DSM-II) standing as "normal."

The claim has always been that "new" evidence revealed that homosexuality was normal, when in fact, nothing had changed, and we were witnessing to another capitulation to the whims of Satan.

Dr. Charles Socarides, writing in *Sexual Politics and Scientific Logic: The Issue of Homosexuality* stated: "To declare a condition a 'non-condition,' a group of practitioners had removed it from our list of serious psychosexual disorders. The action was all the more remarkable when one considers that it involved an out-of-hand and peremptory disregard and dismissal not only of hundreds of psychiatric and psychoanalytic research papers and reports, but also a number of other serious studies by groups of psychiatrists, psychologists, and educators over the past seventy years..."

Now before I am labeled as a homophobe, I want to encourage you to read my Internet article "Does God Love Homosexuals?" In same, I express that I believe, based on Scripture, that God does love us all, but will not tolerate disobedience. For example, He will not abide adultery on the part of heterosexuals. People in love with the worldly are His enemy, meaning a practicing homosexual will not enter the Kingdom.

> Do you not know that the unrighteous will not inherit the kingdom of God? Do not be deceived. Neither fornicators, nor idolaters, nor adulterers, nor homosexuals, nor sodomites, nor thieves, nor covetous, nor drunkards, nor revilers, nor extortionists will inherit the kingdom of God.
> (1 Corinthians 6:9-10)

Clearly God doesn't single out the homosexual; we all have standards we must obey or suffer the consequences.

As for those who claim homosexuality is not a choice, that they are born that way, it's a straw-man argument, because it doesn't matter (although it has yet to be proven). We know scientifically that some people are more prone to violence, to alcoholism, drugs, etc., but that doesn't relieve them of the responsibility to conduct themselves in a manner approved by society. And just like a man with the alcoholism gene is not allowed to drive drunk or a man prone to violence is not allowed to beat his wife, there are spiritual consequences for those who ignore God's commandments regarding sexual behavior—heterosexual or homosexual.

But the homosexual lobby wants what it wants, and it will not stop until they get their way, even if that means bringing down America with it.

Question: If homosexuality is "normal" and healthy as the homosexual lobby claims, then sexual statistics for both the heterosexual and homosexual should be somewhat alike within certain parameters, but they're not.

Let's start with the number of sexual partners of the homosexual in their average lifetime. One study states the following. "Prior to the AIDS epidemic, a 1978 study found:

- 75% of white, gay males claimed to have had more than 100 lifetime male sex partners
- 15% claimed 100-249 sex partners
- 17% claimed 250-499
- 15% claimed 500-999
- 28% claimed more than 1,000 lifetime male sex partners

Levels of promiscuity subsequently declined, but some observers are concerned that promiscuity is again approaching the levels of the 1970s. The medical consequence of this promiscuity is that gays have a greatly increased likelihood of contracting HIV/AIDS, syphilis and other STDs." While the original study was from the late 1970s, the article it is taken from is from 2002. (Dr. J.R. Diggs, Jr., M.D., "The Health Risks of Gay Sex." Corporate Resource Council [2002]) Other more recent studies suggest the total overall average is 200+ per lifetime.

I am sure that there are heterosexuals who have an equal number of lifetime sexual partners, but most will probably agree that the average for heterosexual people is far less, which helps explains the disparity between the percentage of AIDS victims between homosexuals and heterosexuals. As of 2001, sixty-four% of men with AIDS were men who had sex with other men. According to the CDC, bi-sexual men are the conduit to the heterosexual community.

The more sexual partners people have, the more likely that they'll end up with a sexually transmitted disease. This has always been true. For example, according to *The Archives of Internal Medicine*, homosexuals contract syphilis at a rate ten times that of heterosexuals. These facts would lead a rational person to surmise that homosexuality is not normal, and most certainly is not healthy.

If homosexuality is normal, as the pro-homosexual lobby would have us believe, this wouldn't be true: WASHINGTON, DC, June 6, 2005 (LifeSiteNews.com) – A new study which analyzed tens of thousands of gay obituaries and compared them with AIDS deaths data from the Centers for Disease Control (CDC) has shown that the life expectancy for homosexuals is about twenty years shorter than that of the general public. The study, entitled "Gay obituaries closely track officially reported deaths from AIDS" has been published in *Psychological Reports* (2005;96:693-697) This is from an article entitled <u>Yet Another Study Confirms Gay Life Expectancy 20 Years Shorter.</u>

This is one aspect of the homosexual lifestyle those on the Progressive Left refuse to acknowledge. God warns us regarding homosexuality—not to make us feel guilty, but to save us.

> Yet do not count [him] as an enemy, but admonish [him] as a brother.
> (2 Thessalonians 3:15)

We Christians reach out to our homosexual brothers to save them as God instructs. It goes back to the principle explained in my child-in-the-street analogy. We admonish them, not to harm them, but to save them from traffic.

> He who spares the rod hates his son, But he who loves him disciplines him promptly.
> (Proverbs 13:24)

Pay particular attention to when the words "hates" and "loves" are applied. And while I am sure homosexuals bristle at being called children, we are all children to God, notwithstanding our sexual orientation.

If we Christians hated homosexuals (as they apparently believe), we would say nothing and let them destroy themselves. Our love for them is evident in the slings and arrows that come our way, because we try and help.

I'd like to comment on the fact that I don't use the term "gays," but instead opt for the more accurate term "homosexual." I do this, because I refuse to fall into the trap of the Progressives, who constantly play semantic games with words to hide their agenda and sometimes awful truths.

"You are of [your] father the devil, and the desires of your father you want to do. He was a murderer from the beginning,
and does not stand in the truth, because there is no truth in
him. When he speaks a lie, he speaks from his own [resources],
for he is a liar and the father of it.
(John 8:44)

Using Language to Hide an Agenda

Which is why homosexuals have become "gay." The abortion
movement became "pro-choice." Radical feminists, who believe that
consensual sex between married partners is a form of rape, have somehow become "victims." Obamacare was turned in The Affordable Care
Act, when a more proper description would be the Not Affordable
Care Act. And why adultery, the scourge of the family, has been made
to be laughed at in sitcoms and movies, while those who believe in
fidelity are made to feel foolish and "out-of-touch."

That's why Barbara Walters, a TV icon, was cheered by her fans
on her latest book tour promoting a book wherein she proudly lets the
world know that she had an affair with a married senator. The list goes
on and on. The point is, those opposing God always use language to
hide the reality of matters. "Gay" brings another context to mind than
does the word: homosexual.

By the way, for those who have bought the homosexual agenda,
and therefore see homosexuality as normal and healthy, I want to urge
you to read the homosexual sex manual of your choice. I will not quote
any of the practices here, as it would be inappropriate and abhorrent
to me personally.

That said, homosexual practices turn the stomachs of most heterosexuals. They are so foul that when a congressman attempted to read
from such a manual on the floor of the House of Representatives he
was stopped and admonished. It's similar to the pro-abortion lobby
stopping ads that show a real abortion.

Supposedly both abortion and homosexuality are "normal," but the practice(s) of both must never see the light of day, because those in charge know that if the average American ever sees what we're actually talking about, abortion will be outlawed and the rapidly forward moving homosexual agenda will grind to an immediate halt.

Civil Rights

One of the devices of the Progressive Left's homosexual agenda is to turn the deviancy into a civil right, because all American's believe and support civil rights. But comparing the homosexual movement to the rights of black Americans is just plain wrong.

Those seeking homosexual marriage say that "restricting" marriage to one man and one woman is discriminatory and unfair. How exactly? The law is applied to everyone exactly the same: any man may marry any woman and vice-versa. And no man may marry another man. Legally, where's the discrimination? Everyone is treated the same.

The "problem" is the homosexuals want special rights that violate the law. So the law is being changed, and not for the betterment of America. For those who see this as "just" a religious/Christian issue, I remind that there are hundreds of non-Christian countries that have the same laws in principle regarding marriage as DOMA. Clearly, other peoples believe that making marriage into something it was never intended to be is not in their society's best interest.

But clear thinking is no longer the crux of the homosexual issue, as we've stopped being able to think rationally in order to be PC and intellectually tolerant. For example, most right- thinking people correctly condemned the scandal in the Catholic Church regarding priests sexually abusing young altar boys. It is a stain on the church that will perhaps never be made clean. If we are to learn from history, that might be in the best interests of the church in order to ensure such atrocities never recur.

Of course, as the Progressives are wont to do, they attack the church regarding this matter at every turn, as if the sinful priests can bring down the church (which they cannot do).

However, equally important is the church's hierarchy trying to cover up the scandal for decades. Without beating this to death, I bring it up for this reason: the very same people hounding the church are the same ones who champion the "rights" of openly homosexual Boy Scouts and potential Scout leaders. They say that gay Scouts and leaders poise no potential threat to heterosexual Scouts, as homosexual boys/men are just as in control of their urges as heterosexual men. The number of homosexual sexual partners we talked about earlier would seem to call that conclusion into question. And who do these people think were molesting the altar boys? Straight men or homosexual men/priests? In a general sense (and there have to be exceptions) homosexual men cannot be trusted to be alone with young boys. That is a historically proven fact, and no amount of burying our heads in the sand of political correctness will change that.

When logic no longer has sway in a political debate, those advocating a new "tolerant" position have won. In this case, it's the homosexuals and those who support them.

And what does God have to say?

Note: The following Scriptures apply to practicing homosexuals. Non-practicing homosexuals and those who have repented and accepted Christ into their lives will be treated like any other Christian on their way to heaven.

So God created man in His [own] image; in the image of God He created him; male and female He created them.
(Genesis 1:27).

And they called to Lot and said to him, "Where are the men who came to you tonight? Bring them out to us that we may know them [carnally]." So Lot went out to them through the doorway, shut the door behind him, and said, "Please, my brethren, do not do so wickedly!
(Genesis 19:5-7).

'You shall not lie with a male as with a woman. It [is] an abomination.
(Leviticus 18:22).

'If a man lies with a male as he lies with a woman, both of them have committed an abomination. They shall surely be put to death. Their blood [shall be] upon them.
(Leviticus 20:13).

And there were also perverted persons in the land. They did according to all the abominations of the nations, which the LORD had cast out before the children of Israel.
(1 Kings 14:24).

And he banished the perverted persons from the land, and removed all the idols that his fathers had made.
(1 Kings 15:12).

And He answered and said to them, "Have you not read that He who made [them] at the beginning 'made them male and female,'" and said, "For this reason a man shall leave his father and mother and be joined to his wife, and the two shall become one flesh?"
(Matthew 19:4-5).

Therefore God also gave them up to uncleanness, in the lusts of their hearts, to dishonor their bodies among themselves, who exchanged the truth of God for the lie, and worshiped and served the creature rather than the Creator, who is blessed forever. Amen. For this reason God gave them up to vile passions. For even their women exchanged the natural use for what is against nature. Likewise also the men, leaving the natural use of the woman, burned in their lust for one another, men with men committing what is shameful,

and receiving in themselves the penalty of their error which was due.
(Romans 1:24-27).

Do you not know that the unrighteous will not inherit the kingdom of God? Do not be deceived. Neither fornicators, nor idolaters, nor adulterers, nor homosexuals, nor sodomites, nor thieves, nor covetous, nor drunkards, nor revilers, nor extortionists will inherit the kingdom of God.
(1 Corinthians 6:9-10).

Now the works of the flesh are evident, which are: adultery, fornication, uncleanness, lewdness, idolatry, sorcery, hatred, contentions, jealousies, outbursts of wrath, selfish ambitions, dissensions, heresies, envy, murders, drunkenness, revelries, and the like; of which I tell you beforehand, just as I also told [you] in time past, that those who practice such things will not inherit the kingdom of God.
(Galatians 5:19-21).

But fornication and all uncleanness or covetousness, let it not even be named among you, as is fitting for saints; neither filthiness, nor foolish talking, nor coarse jesting, which are not fitting, but rather giving of thanks. For this you know, that no fornicator, unclean person, nor covetous man, who is an idolater, has any inheritance in the kingdom of Christ and God. Let no one deceive you with empty words, for because of these things the wrath of God comes upon the sons of disobedience. Therefore do not be partakers with them.
(Ephesians 5:3-7).

Therefore put to death your members, which are on the earth: fornication, uncleanness, passion, evil desire, and covetousness, which is idolatry. Because of these things the wrath of God is

coming upon the sons of disobedience,
(Colossians 3:5-7).

But we know that the law [is] good if one uses it lawfully, knowing this: that the law is not made for a righteous person, but for [the] lawless and insubordinate, for [the] ungodly and for sinners, for [the] unholy and profane, for murderers of fathers and murderers of mothers, for manslayers, or fornicators, for sodomites, for kidnappers, for liars, for perjurers, and if there is any other thing that is contrary to sound doctrine, according to the glorious gospel of the blessed God, which was committed to my trust.
(1 Timothy 1:8-11).

They profess to know God, but in works they deny [Him], being abominable, disobedient, and disqualified for every good work.
(Titus 1:16).

But there shall by no means enter it anything that defiles, or causes an abomination or a lie, but only those who are written in the Lamb's Book of Life.
(Revelation 21:27).

Before wrapping this chapter up, I want to bring to your attention an important distinction that too often people miss as they defend their homosexual lifestyle or their Progressive Liberal political position that includes making homosexuality "normal."

So much of what the Bible says about homosexuality is applicable to homosexual *and* heterosexuals alike. While homosexuality is mentioned specifically in Scriptures, it is also referred to as an abomination because it's fornication.

Both homosexuals *and* heterosexuals fornicate, and both (some) practice sodomy, so God is most certainly *not* picking on the homosexual. Further, notwithstanding certain states and the Supreme Court's recent ruling(s), as a sexual practice, only heterosexuals can be guilty of adultery in the normal understanding of the relationship. Yes, some homosexuals are guilty, too, as they have sex with married males, but that is only a small percentage of the problem.

The point is, the homosexual lobby likes to paint themselves as victims (biblically), as it helps them further their agenda, but the truth is, there are just as many rules for heterosexuals. And if heterosexuals ignore the rules, they will receive the same punishment as disobedient homosexuals.

Ask yourself, are the positions of our society and the positions of the Lord on abortion and homosexuality compatible? Are there any areas of agreement? The answer, of course, is no. There is *no* common ground.

There are many other issues we could examine, but the point should be made. For instance, radical feminism. They most adamantly will not accept God's will.

Wives, submit to your own husbands, as to the Lord.
(Ephesians 5:22)

Or the hideous American-welfare system that has spent over seven trillion dollars since beginning the War on Poverty with nothing to show for it except that there are more people in poverty under President Obama than there were under President Johnson (the War's father)

Why hasn't it worked? Why has it kept the underclass in perpetual financial slavery? Because we, as a nation, ignored God's commandment.

For even when we were with you, we commanded you this:
If anyone will not work, neither shall he eat.
(2 Thessalonians 3:10)

The Bible is replete with the command to feed the needy and help them, but our current welfare system has long since lost its direction as generation after generation now see their "job" to be on welfare and do whatever they can to increase their benefits. We have millions of people who could work, but won't. They should go hungry, as the Bible says.

Again we could review topic after topic, all with the same conclusion: God and our society are no longer compatible. As we talked earlier, light and darkness cannot exist in the same space at the same time—neither can the new America and God.

The only plausible answer is: one has to be done away with, as God's Word convicts us, and we don't like it, not one bit.

We're forward-thinking, Progressive, tolerant, and God just gets in the way of us doing what we want, when we want—on a personal and governmental level. God makes us feel guilty, and we crave being comfortable in our sin. If God's around, that's not going to happen. He must be destroyed. But how?

3

HOW CAN YOU KILL A GOD WHO CANNOT BE KILLED?

Surely it has occurred to you that in Killing God we have a tactical problem. I earlier went to great lengths to explain how truly powerful God is, which is why society must destroy Him. And now we're discussing *how* to kill Him. At this point, the subject must seem disjointed and incongruous, so a quick preface to this chapter is required.

Question: If a tree falls in a forest, and there's no one around to hear it fall, does it make a sound?

Quite clearly a sound is a sound, and if one doubts the obvious, had there been a recording devise left in the forest one could later play the sound. Then too, a sound produces a sound wave that plants and animals would hear whether or not a human hears.

But the question has relevance.

The relevance: we humans see everything through the prism of what we can see and hear. Abstracts are only understood by a few. Theoretical concepts by fewer still. If this were not true the question about a sound in the forest would have no meaning whatsoever. But the mere hypothesis of the question puts into place a hierarchical consideration of the importance of man. Without man even provable sound does not necessarily exists (or so man believes).

Let's try this. Here are the lyrics to the iconic folk song, *Puff the Magic Dragon*:

THE PLOT TO KILL GOD

Puff, the magic dragon lived by the sea
And frolicked in the autumn mist in a land called Honah Lee,
Little Jackie paper loved that rascal puff,
And brought him strings and sealing wax and other fancy stuff. oh

Puff, the magic dragon lived by the sea
And frolicked in the autumn mist in a land called Honah Lee,
Puff, the magic dragon lived by the sea
And frolicked in the autumn mist in a land called Honah Lee.

Together they would travel on a boat with billowed sail
Jackie kept a lookout perched on puffs gigantic tail,
Noble kings and princes would bow whenever they came,
Pirate ships would lower their flag when puff roared out his name. oh!

Puff, the magic dragon lived by the sea
And frolicked in the autumn mist in a land called Honah Lee,
Puff, the magic dragon lived by the sea
And frolicked in the autumn mist in a land called Honah Lee.

A dragon lives forever but not so little boys
Painted wings and giant rings make way for other toys.
One grey night it happened, Jackie paper came no more
And puff that mighty dragon, he ceased his fearless roar.

His head was bent in sorrow, green scales fell like rain,
Puff no longer went to play along the cherry lane.
Without his life-long friend, puff could not be brave,
So puff that mighty dragon sadly slipped into his cave. oh!

Puff, the magic dragon lived by the sea
And frolicked in the autumn mist in a land called Honah Lee,
Puff, the magic dragon lived by the sea
And frolicked in the autumn mist in a land called Honah Lee.

HOW CAN YOU KILL A GOD WHO CANNOT BE KILLED?

(Written by: Leonard Lipton & Peter Yarrow. Inspired by: Ogden Nash's poem "Custard the Dragon." Performed by: Peter Paul & Mary, 1962. www.lyricsfreak.com)

Please don't for a moment think I am in any manner, shape, or form comparing *Puff the Magic Dragon* to our loving God, because I'm not. What I am doing, however, is using the song to make a point.

When did Puff cease to be what he had always been? When Jackie no longer had time for him, that's when. When Jackie grew up, as we grow up.

Be honest, when you were a child and were first introduced to Jesus, wasn't your faith all-encompassing? While you may have had questions, they weren't questions regarding God's existence, rather a heartfelt need to want to know God and His Son better. But as we grew older, other things starting taking away our God-time, and we attended church less and less. We stopped reading our Bible. And then we stopped obeying the Bible, as we needed to go along to get along. Such are the pressures of life.

No, Puff isn't a song about God, but it does reflect an important principle that explains what happens to our belief system as we grow older.

Puff disappeared back into his cave when Jackie unilaterally curtailed their relationship. God will always be, but as He pertains to the single individual, He too ceases to exist when we remove Him from our lives and culture.

Notwithstanding how you may view her politics, it is worthy to study what the Progressives and their willing accomplices (the media) did to Sarah Palin. It also is pertinent to this chapter.

Palin, regardless of what you thought of her personally, was a success in her political endeavors. She went from being a small-town mayor in Alaska to the Governor of the State, and in the process cemented her position as one of the most powerful woman politicians in the world. Yet, because she was from Alaska, she was not that well-known, regardless of her power and success. When John McCain announced her as his running mate, to much of America the following was asked: Who?

Her relative anonymity played well for the Progressive Left, because it allowed them to define her to the voting populous—with, of course, the help of the media. They filled the news void about Ms. Palin, not with facts, but with political animus designed to further not the truth, but their leftist agenda. She was a woman, who presented a problem for the Left; they didn't want to offend half the voters (women), but as we soon found out, the Left and the media, including The National Organization of Women, only care about women who are Progressives.

Simply put, if those on the Right had called Hillary Clinton what the Left called Sarah Palin the world would have come to an end. More importantly, if the Right had painted Mrs. Clinton as an ignorant buffoon incapable of stringing together enough words to make a sentence with meaning, the charges of misogyny would have drowned out any serious dialog. Mrs. Palin had a lot going for her, but was destroyed by people making fun of her and spreading unfounded rumors about everything possible, including her special-needs son.

What was done to her was despicable.

We could go reviewing example after example of how the Progressive Left works, but hopefully it's not necessary, as they all would have at their core the *Rules for Radicals* written by the late communist organizer Saul Alinsky.

Alinsky is the father of the Community Organizer Movement. His entire belief system is based on the premise that the ends justify the means, with the ends being the acquisition of power. Alinsky was a humanist to the end. A higher power was not in his equation for mankind. The masses, right or wrong, are to prevail for the world to be right in his eyes and those of his sycophantic followers, such as our president.

Whatever you might think of Mr. Alinsky and his political perversions, he was good at what he did, and we must give the devil his due.

He believed any political movement had to have a common enemy, and if there isn't one, one is to be created. Once isolated and subsequently targeted his Rules are to be applied in a take-no-prisoners fashion.

The Rules

1. "Power is not only what you have, but what the enemy thinks you have."
2. "Never go outside the expertise of your people."
3. "Whenever possible, go outside the expertise of the enemy."
4. "Make the enemy live up to its own book of rules."
5. "Ridicule is man's most potent weapon."
6. "A good tactic is one your people enjoy."
7. "A tactic that drags on too long becomes a drag."
8. "Keep the pressure on. Never let up."
9. "The threat is usually more terrifying than the thing itself."
10. "The major premise for tactics is the development of operations that will maintain a constant pressure upon the opposition."
11. "If you push a negative hard enough, it will push through and become a positive."
12. "The price of a successful attack is a constructive alternative."
13. "Pick the target, freeze it, personalize it, and polarize it." (Source: www.unionfreeamerica.com)

Let's apply each "rule" to the politics of the day to see how they have been ingrained into our consciousness without fanfare and are now accepted as undeniable fact.

1. "Power is not only what you have, but what the enemy thinks you have."

The membership of N.O.W. has been declining for years, but if you listen to the news media you'd think they represent every woman in America.

Cindy Shehan was given an air of power regarding war in the Middle East. Every time she picketed George Bush's Texas White House, she got wall-to-wall coverage from all the major networks, even though her protest usually consisted of about ten people.

The Left constantly tells us there is a consensus among scientists that global warming is a fact that will destroy the planet. Seldom are they ever challenged regarding their "facts." This gives them a position of authority, notwithstanding there is no such consensus and the earth has been in a holding pattern of cooling temperature for a decade and a half. Then too, in order to cover the fact that global warming is no longer happening, the movement changed its name to "climate change." BTW, for those older reading this, we can remember being told by the experts when we were kids that we'd all die because of the coming ice age.

There are thousands of groups that spring up overnight to give authority to whatever agenda they champion, and they all have very official sounding names even though they represent few actual people. The news media loves these groups, because they give credibility to their leftist positions that would otherwise rightfully be seen as ludicrous.

2. "Never go outside the expertise of your people."

Progressives pick a subject and/or target and stick to it. It allows them to focus their efforts while making themselves as small a target as possible. They attack one target/person at a time; it's their way of getting the biggest bang for the buck. When I was in junior high school I submitted to my history teacher that I wanted to do a paper on the Civil War. He correctly informed me that a topic that large, with that many ramifications, could not be summarized in tens pages or less. He suggested a paper on one battle of the war, which is what I did. I've never forgotten the lesson that a broad-based approach to any subject hardly ever works, because it can't. On the other hand, focusing on one aspect or subject, quickly made you an expert on the subject and better able to control the discussion.

Yes, Progressives have something to say on everything, but they have different groups and/or spokespersons for each topic. That's why their people always seem better prepared than those in opposition.

3. "Whenever possible, go outside the expertise of the enemy."

This is obviously an extension of rule #2, albeit from another direction. Simply put, find the weakness in the opposition and then exploit it, while in the process making them look like people who should not be listened to, much less believed. You want to know the subject better than they do, while, when possible, expanding the subject beyond their knowledge and expertise.

It's kind of a bait-and-switch technique; have you ever watched a Sunday morning talk show that features a Progressive and a Conservative. Invariably the Progressive will expand or change the subject, with the help of their sympathetic host, so that they are no longer talking about the advertised subject, but a topic that makes the Conservative look bad while making the Leftist look good.

For instance, after the George Zimmerman trial in Florida, whenever the acquittal is discussed the Left changes the subject from the fact that the trial was fair in all respects, to the jury lacked sympathy for the Martin family. And they immediately win the argument (as who among us cannot feel the pain the Martins must feel regarding the loss of their young son), while making the person representing the Right look like a hard-hearted imbecile. And then the entire white race is made to look like racists, because, after all, the jury was all white (actually one woman was Hispanic, but much like Mr. Zimmerman, was called a "white" Hispanic (whatever that is). This is a winning strategy employed by the Left for decades.

4. "Make the enemy live up to its own book of rules."

This is one of my favorites and explains, in part, why the Democrats get a pass for the very same event(s) that Republicans are excoriated for—to the point that they usually are made to leave office. For example, sex scandals.

When a Republican is caught in a sex scandal at any level of government, they are hounded out of office. Usually by Republicans, even if no law has been broken. That's not to say they shouldn't be held accountable, as we should be served by men and woman of honor, not those who abuse their power for personal, and in this case, sexual gain. After an appropriate amount of news coverage, the Republican hierarchy usually goes to the offender and explains they must resign to spare the party anymore shame and embarrassment. Usually the offender complies.

On the other hand, when a Democrat does the same thing, in actuality or principle, we're told this is a private matter and in no way hinders the offender's ability to serve their constituency. And this is true even if the Democrat offender has broken the law. Witness Elliot Spitzer. Yes, he lost his governorship, but he has never been held legally accountable for his violation of law, and he was immediately given a job in the media by the willingly complaint Left-leaning news outlets. As of this writing, he's now running for office in the state he betrayed.

Why the difference in treatment? Easy—the media champions the Democrats, while taking every opportunity to do harm to the Republicans. They are unconcerned with their obvious hypocrisy.

And here's where Rule #4 comes into play. The Dems and the media say that the reason for disparity in coverage is that Republicans are always talking about and pushing a "Family Values" agenda, while the Dems don't. They mean the Republicans are hypocrites and therefore have to be exposed as such. Yes, people who espouse a certain belief ought to hold themselves to the same standard. That said, because someone fails to do so doesn't mean their point of view does not hold merit. Conversely, just because a person doesn't espouse a certain set of values doesn't mean they should not be held accountable and/or get a pass for violating existing law.

One thing we can all agree on is, Rule #4 works.

5. "Ridicule is man's most potent weapon."

This is the Progressive Left's most potent tool, just as advertised. They know if you can make someone, anyone, appear to be a clown, it no longer matters what they say or do; they're finished.

Before Sarah Palin there was Dan Quayle. Senator Quayle was tapped as the VP candidate for the Republican Party at the convention that nominated George H.W. Bush the elder. He became the nation's Vice President when Bush defeated Michael Dukakis and Lloyd Bentsen. He had a long history of service to the country and was one of our nation's most active V.P.s. As he was an active Conservative, he was despised by the Left and needed to be politically destroyed, lest he run for the presidency at a later date.

At a campaign stop at a middle-school, the Left and its media representatives got what they needed. His most famous error occurred when he changed 12-year old student William Figueroa's correct spelling (Quayle was judging a spelling bee) of "potato" to "potatoe." He was visiting the Muñoz Rivera Elementary School in Trenton, New Jersey, on June 15, 1992. Quayle was lambasted for his apparent inability to spell the word "potato." According to the *New York Times* and Quayle's published memoirs, he was relying on cards provided by the school, which Quayle claims included the misspelling. Quayle said he was uncomfortable with the spelling he gave, but did so because he trusted the school's incorrect written materials instead of his own judgment.

Vice President Quayle was a master of the malapropism and misstatement, of that there can be no doubt. But he was a good man who did his job, of that too there can be no doubt.

For those who say Mr. Quayle was not intellectually fit to hold public office, much less of the higher variety, let's see how the Left and the press treat Vice President Joe Biden and his misstatements. Here are just a few compiled by Daniel Kurtzman:

"I mean, you got the first mainstream African-American, who is articulate and bright and clean and a nice-looking guy. I mean, that's a storybook, man." –Joe Biden, referring to Barack Obama at the beginning of the 2008 Democratic primary campaign, Jan. 31, 2007

"A man I'm proud to call my friend. A man who will be the next President of the United States — Barack America!" --Joe Biden, at his first campaign rally with Barack Obama after being announced as his running mate, Springfield, Ill., Aug. 23, 2008

"Stand up, Chuck, let 'em see ya." --Joe Biden, to Missouri state Sen. Chuck Graham, who is in a wheelchair, Columbia, Missouri, Sept. 12, 2008

"When the stock market crashed, Franklin D. Roosevelt got on the television and didn't just talk about the, you know, the princes of greed. He said, 'Look, here's what happened.'" –Joe Biden, apparently unaware that FDR wasn't president when the stock market crashed in 1929 and that only experimental TV sets were in use at that time, interview with Katie Couric, Sept. 22, 2008

"Look, John's last-minute economic plan does nothing to tackle the number-one job facing the middle class, and it happens to be, as Barack says, a three-letter word: jobs. J-O-B-S, jobs." --Joe Biden, Athens, Ohio, Oct. 15, 2008

"This is a big f---king deal!" --Joe Biden, caught on an open mic congratulating President Barack Obama during the health-care signing ceremony, Washington, D.C., March 23, 2010

And what is the press's reaction to Vice President Biden's gaffs? "Oh, it's just Joe being Joe." Remember now, Vice President Quayle was called an idiot and worse for far less, but while the press ruined Dan Quayle's life, they ran interference for the Democrats, especially President Obama. Here are a few of his gaffs, again compiled by Daniel Kurtzman:

"No, no. I have been practicing...I bowled a 129. It's like -- it was like Special Olympics, or something." –making an off-hand joke during an appearance on "The Tonight Show," March 19, 2009

"What I was suggesting –you're absolutely right that John McCain has not talked about my Muslim faith..." –in an interview with ABC's George Stephanopoulos, who jumped in to correct Obama by saying "your Christian faith," which Obama quickly clarified.

"Just this past week, we passed out of the U.S. Senate Banking Committee -- which is my committee -- a bill to call for divestment from Iran as way of ratcheting up the pressure to ensure that they don't obtain a nuclear weapon." --referring to a committee he is not on,

Sderot, Israel, July 23, 2008

"On this Memorial Day, as our nation honors its unbroken line of fallen heroes -- and I see many of them in the audience here today -- our sense of patriotism is particularly strong."

"I've now been in 57 states –I think one left to go." --at a campaign event in Beaverton, Oregon.

The point of this exercise is not to make light of our President and Vice President - rather it's to show that those in both parties make mistakes, and say things they wish they could take back. While that's true, something else is true; those on the Left always, and I mean always, will use something a politician says or does that calls into question their intellect, and use it to make them out to be a clown not worthy of our vote—that is, unless they're a left-leaning Democrat.

6. "A good tactic is one your people enjoy."

Have you ever noticed how the Left is so adept at dicing and slicing a political issue, how they can find an angle that works to their advantage, how they can find "dirt" on a political opponent that destroys her, and therefore their position in the debate.

Progressives l-o-v-e this tactic. They have honed it to an art form. They are good at destroying others because they're so good at it - or is it they're so good at, because they enjoy it?

They're good at demonstrations, which they have adored since the Civil Rights movement of the 1960s.

They're good at debating issues by not debating issues. They instead change the subject to something they want to talk about.

And they're exceptionally good at "group think" and are the acknowledged masters of "talking points." When they want to get their points in front of the public, they all do so at every opportunity; a reporter can ask a Democrat how they're enjoying the weather, and they'll get a five-minute dissertation on why the Republicans want to poison our air and water and starve little children. And while they're doing so, every other Democrat will be delivering the same message regardless of the forum and/or question they're asked.

Progressives have a most distinct pattern; it's one they enjoy and are, giving the devil his due, the very best at it.

7. "A tactic that drags on too long becomes a drag."

This is one of the Rules that the Left has a little trouble with. They often fail to understand that many Americans get tired of their leftist antics. I'm seventy now, and I can tell you I've heard the same things over and over ad-nauseum, but in fairness, when something works why change it? And let's face it, and it pains me to say so, the Left is better at politics than those of conservative persuasion (ignore the RINOs) - that's why there are so many of them and so few of us.

And why can you no longer tell the difference between the two parties? They have morphed into one party that has as its objective: holding onto their personal power and wealth.

Have you ever wondered that virtually all politicians serving in Washington are millionaires, not withstanding that their salaries are small when compared to a CEO's salary? Some arrive in D.C. as middle-class citizens, and in a few years they are millionaires. Hmmm?

Have you ever wondered why our "leaders" exempt themselves from the laws they pass? The laws the rest of us must obey?

Have you ever wondered why Washington has bankrupted Social Security, but their retirement benefits, which are far superior to ours, are completely and totally funded?

Have you ever wondered why The Affordable Care Act exempts those in Congress? Gee, if it's as good as they say it is, you'd think they'd want to be onboard.

This Rule should probably be changed to insert the word "topic" for tactic.

8. "Keep the pressure on. Never let up."

Those on the Left jump from one "crisis" to another. In fact, even for those who follow politics, it's hard to keep up with their latest disaster. Or at least what they call a disaster. They really don't want the masses to be able to think straight, so the politicians can do whatever they want without interference.

And they want to have more and more people dependent on government at all levels. It's gotten so bad now that there are millions of people looking to Washington to do something about the weather, the economy, our healthcare, and the raising of our children.

Remember, these are the same people who run the Department of Motor Vehicles, the IRS, and our out-of-money Social Security System. And most importantly, these are the people who ran up seventeen-trillion dollars of debt to ensure they were reelected.

By the way, do you know what a trillion dollars is? It's a thousand billions. A billion is a thousand millions. Also, while we are told we owe seventeen-trillion dollars (which can never be repaid), the truth is the real amount, considering all debt and contingent liabilities, is somewhere (and this is as close as anyone can come) near one-hundred thirty-trillion dollars.

So it's easy to see why we "should" turn to Washington for answers; their track record speaks for itself.

Yes, they never let up. One of the offshoots of this pressure policy is the government creates a problem, entirely of its making, and then tells everyone that we have to give them more power to solve the problem they created. Witness the housing bubble that gutted the stock market. The market collapse was created by the policy of Congress that every American should have the house of their choosing, even if they had no realistic way of paying their monthly mortgage.

Banks were forced to make mortgage loans they knew were bad, but unless they complied with the edicts of the Democrats in control, they would be punished in every way imaginable. So the banks, to their discredit, capitulated, and what we all knew was going to happen, happened.

If you'll remember, when it hit the fan, we were told we had to do something major within hours or America was doomed, when, of course, it was not. This con garnered Congress immense additional power to dole out monetary goodies to their cohorts. In short, they created the problem, and then rode to our "rescue."

Lastly on this subject, we spent trillions of dollars in President Obama's stimulus package to only have three things happen:

1. We substantially added to the national debt.
2. It didn't do what we were promised it would do, as our economy has yet to improve.
3. No one knows where the money went. No one!

I'm not joking, millions, billions, trillions of dollars just disappeared. Not one federal agency has ever been able to account for what happened. The money is just gone. Poof!

9. "The threat is usually more terrifying than the thing itself."

To a Progressive, everything is a crisis that must be solved yesterday, or the sky will fall. Causing panic among the masses ensures no one will have time to think and debate matters. Progressives, who normally create the problems, then say they can fix things. Voters who are now so dependent on government then demand government do something --even if it's wrong!

Remember the most recent stock market crash? Our imploding financial base needed trillions to be spent as the Progressives deemed prudent --even though the Liberals caused the problem.

In the aftermath of 9/11 both Dems and Republicans voted for "safety" measures, which also took away much of our freedoms and gave us long lines at airports supervised by workers hired, given a few months training, and then were hailed as homeland-security experts.

Or how about the student-loan crisis? The "crisis" was that those who'd borrowed great sums to go to college were being asked to honor their commitments.

And my favorites: healthcare and illegal immigration. Healthcare was such a crisis that Congress passed a monstrous bill that no one read until it was too late. Our then Speaker of the House, the person 3rd in line for the presidency, said "We have to pass the bill so you can find out what is in it, away from the fog of the controversy" (Source: www.hyscience.com). And we all sat and did nothing. And immigration? Well, illegals have rights, and we have to do something right this instant, or the whole world will collapse. It's not fair that they're treated as they are, they deserve benefits, even benefits that most Americans don't qualify for.

No matter how you feel about the amnesty bill we're now debating, it should be moot. Why? Because we're broke and can't afford one more mouth at the table. America considering making legal another 11 to 30 million citizens is financial suicide.

Some believe that bringing illegal aliens into the fold via amnesty will somehow strengthen our economy. If that's true, which it's not, why not open our boarders and let 50 million people in?

Honestly, the arguments of the Progressives are ludicrous on face value, which is why then need to create panic so bills get passed before anyone reads them.

The list of crisises during the last 10-20 years is too long to recount here, but even if we can't remember them all, they are voluminous, and they all have one thing in common: the Progressives use panic to get what they want.

Every once in awhile the Progressives let aspects of their plans slip out. Witness the Mayor of Chicago, Rahm Emanuel, while still Chief of Staff of the Obama Administration, when he said, "You never want a serious crisis to go to waste. And what I mean by that is an opportunity to do things you think you could not do before."

I'm sure many politicians of like mind wished he'd never been so open, because he became like the Wizard of Oz who said, "Pay no attention to the man behind the curtain." Look closely at virtually every political crisis in America, and there's a Progressive trying to use it to their political advantage.

Yes, there are legitimate crisises, but mostly they require thought, not panic. Those advocating panic have another agenda in mind, and it has little to do with their self-created hysteria or solving real problems.

10. "The major premise for tactics is the development of operations that will maintain a constant pressure upon the opposition."

As I mentioned, I am 70 years old.
Consider what the Bible says.

I said, 'Age should speak, And multitude of years should teach wisdom.'
(Job 32:7)

There are many such sentiments that make clear that people who have lived awhile have seen much, and because of their experience, often should be listened to because they've seen like circumstances that may look new to you, but are old-hat to them.

We have to seek balance in all we do. Progressives don't want to leave that to chance. They want constant pressure on the public and those who oppose them politically. That's why Democrat scandals seems to disappear overnight no matter how serious, while Republican scandals have no end—pressure, constant pressure.

Everything the Progressives do puts pressure on their opposition. I've seen it since I was 16 and became interested in politics. Nothing has changed.

That which has been [is] what will be, That which [is] done is what will be done, And [there is] nothing new under the sun.
(Ecclesiastes 1:9)

The part that saddens me is the American public has yet to catch on that they're being callously manipulated to an end not in their best interest.

Regardless of which end of the political spectrum you're on, we all should be able to agree that America is headed for destruction. We've lost jobs we'll never get back. Our education system is the laughing stock of the free-world, and our economy, viewed through the eyes of a legitimate accounting firm, is bankrupt. By any measure our great nation is headed in the wrong direction, while the ruling elite in Washington are driven to their gated communities in a limo paid for with our money. And while working people can't afford a two-week vacation to anywhere, our President asks us to tighten our belts while he spends 100 million dollars on a trip to Africa that produces absolutely nothing for anyone, except his family.

If you doubt pressure works against your enemies, ask yourself this: do you do better work when you have the time and energy or when you're under a tight deadline and are worried about having enough money to send your child to college?

Even a ballplayer hits better in the early innings than he does in the bottom of the ninth, when his team is behind a run, and there are two outs and two strikes on him. Everything Progressives do is designed to incapacitate their opposition though intimidation and pressure.

For example, remember the last few years of George Bush-the-younger's administration, and gas got over two dollars and then close to three? Every newscast had at its lead story that America could not survive with such high gas prices, something had to be done! The Progressives were calling for congressional investigations! Each day the pressure intensified.

Then President Obama was inaugurated, and gas got to three and then over four dollars. And not a word is ever mention on any major newscast. Pressure on the opposition, or the lack of pressure on themselves, is always used by Progressives.

Another example. During the war in Iraq, the media—almost exclusively a partner with Progressive causes—drummed home the death count of our soldiers. There were pictures of coffins. Lead stories played when certain death-toll milestones were reached. There was coverage of protests, even protests with fewer than ten people attending. Then President Obama was elected, and wars—at least as they pertained to the loss of soldiers—disappeared. No more stories, no more pictures. Once again, the imbalance of pressure.

11. "If you push a negative hard enough, it will push through and become a positive."

This rule can best be explained by looking at the issue of abortion.

When first presented it was something no one really wanted to talk about, but, since there were "back alley" abortions taking place, this was a "solution" everyone could live with. It was a negative subject, no matter how it was approached.

Surely, if Americans knew back then that by now over 50-million abortions would have taken place, Roe v. Wade would have been decided differently. As a society, we would not (back then) have approved such hideous slaughter in such large numbers. So it was sold as a solution to rape and incest, even though the case, as explained earlier, was a fraud.

Over time, those favoring abortion-on-demand, decided that it should be a form of birth control, and abortion was changed to a "woman's right to choose." It took decades, but by using this tactic the negative of abortion was changed to the positive of "women's reproductive rights." Once the radical feminists accomplished the changeover, they became unstoppable, and instead of debating the rights of the innocent unborn, we became solely concerned with the rights of the pregnant woman. There was much she could have done not to become pregnant. But the baby would have to pay the price for the parents' errors in judgment.

For those who are still holding onto the "rape and incest" aspect of the problem, studies show that less than two percent of abortions are a result of these crimes. Compassionate provision needs to be made available (which the pro-life movement offers) for victims; provisions that do not involve killing anyone.

For non-Christians, this is reason enough to allow an abortion. Christians, while most sympathetic to victims of sexual crimes, don't believe, even in cases such as these, that the baby should pay with its life. But for the sake of this discussion, let's not debate the intricacies of the matter, as cases totally less than two percent should not dictate the end-result of ninety-eight percent of the cases.

If you look at many issues of American society through the prism of history, you'll see time and time again that Progressives take negative issues and turn them into a positive that helps them focus and consolidate their power over the lives of the many. Progressives in politics paint themselves as being for the middle-class and poor, yet when you look at their financial statements they are just as rich (if not more so) and removed as any "painted-evil" Conservatives.

One more quick example: America believes the Democrats (Progressives) are the champion of black Americans. Democrats, and Democrats alone, are the reason and cause of the Civil Rights movement. But history says it was the Republicans (Conservatives), who championed civil rights, while the Democrats, especially southern Democrats, did everything in their power to ensure black Americans were treated as if they were still segregated slaves.

By using Rule 11, Progressives have taken their hate for minorities (as witnessed by their opposition to civil rights and the creation of welfare financial slavery) and literally changed history. They have gone from civil rights pariahs to receiving close to one hundred percent political support from the very people they tried to disenfranchise at the ballot box—all because of Rule 11.

12. "The price of a successful attack is a constructive alternative."

This a rule that Conservatives should employ, but they don't, which is why they are so often painted as obstructionists. They know what they don't like and often let it go at that.

This country was founded by men who believed that a government, any government, should (as much as possible) stay out of our lives. Today, we have been politically trained to believe government has the answer to everything, including how to raise our children.

"That government that governs best, governs least"
(Thomas Jefferson?)

"I heartily accept the motto—'That government is best which governs least.'"
Henry David Thoreau (1817-1862)

"The best government is that which governs least."
(John Louis O'Sullivan)

O'Sullivan used those words in the opening editorial for his periodical The United States Magazine and Democratic Review and as the motto of the Review until it ceased publication in 1859.

"The less government we have, the better."
(Ralph Waldo Emerson)

"It is not true that that government is best which is best administered — it is a sophism invented by tyranny to quiet the inquisitive mind; a good administration is at best but a temporary palliative to a bad government, but it does not alter its nature."
(William Penn, founder of Pennsylvania)

"Let us never forget that government is ourselves and not an alien power over us. The ultimate rulers of our democracy are not a President and senators and congressmen and government officials, but the voters of this country."
(Franklin D. Roosevelt)

Based on this comment, I surmise President Roosevelt would be stunned and disappointed to see what modern Democrats have done to the Progressive movement he believed in so deeply.

With each passing generation Progressives have become more active, more intrusive. They have an answer for everything, even questions un-asked.

I am paraphrasing here, but I think it was Barry Goldwater who said, "The first thing we need to do is pass a law that we won't pass another law for ten years. That will give us time to find out where we're really at."

Conservatives often believe that sometimes the best thing for the federal government to do is nothing. That local issues are best served locally. Progressives believe otherwise, which is why we have Roe v. Wade when the Supreme Court made a federal law that constitutionally should have been left to the states.

Progressives know that if they're the party of solutions, even horrid solutions, the opposition will appear to be "do-nothings." Modern America doesn't like do-nothings.

13. "Pick the target, freeze it, personalize it, and polarize it."

This is perhaps the most hideous rule, as it is used to destroy an individual who stands in the way of their agenda. Progressives did it to Dan Quayle and Sarah Palin as we mentioned, but there have been others at all levels of government and social discourse.

Bill and Hillary Clinton labeled it: "The politics of personal destruction," and they were right. The problem with them defining it is they are the acknowledged practitioners of the method, which brings us to an unwritten "rule" of Progressives—whatever you're doing that is illegal and/or immoral, accuse your opposition of the exact same thing *before* they expose you, even if they're right and you're wrong. That way you can say that you're the innocent victim of a smear campaign, because your opponent is just repeating the charges against him against you.

There is so much more I could say about the playbook of

Progressives, but there is no need to, as many books devoted to that singular issue are available.

I would like to sum-up my quick review by saying the bottom-line to the subject is this—for Progressives, the end justifies the means. As liberal politics *is* their religion, how you win doesn't matter. The only thing that matters is if you maintain power, for after all, you're simply trying to do what's best for everyone. That's why in political debates facts seem to mean little to Progressives. They are constantly asking through their stubbornness, "What are you going to believe, me or your lying eyes?" They are dangerous people who epitomize the warning: "The road to hell is paved with good intentions."

I wish Conservatives, and those masquerading as Conservatives, had half the dedication of the Left. They have the courage of their convictions, no matter how wrong, while we run around trying to please groups and the media, who will never see things our way. And in our confusion we have become pitifully weak and ineffective.

Why This Discussion-Here-Now?

I hope at this point some of you are asking yourself—why all the political discussion in a Christian book?

Actually, the answer is painfully simple.

The title of this chapter asks a rhetorical question: "How Can You Kill a God Who Cannot Be Killed?" For non-believers, you cannot kill someone who, in their minds, does not exist, and for true believers God is forever. But, and here's where the two ends of the spectrum meld into the spiritual conflict America faces today, those who believe stand in the way of those who do not believe. Therefore those who believe must be destroyed. And what better way to destroy them than to destroy the God they worship?

Remember now, God's way and the way of the Progressives are *not* compatible and *never* will be. Politicians are always asking smugly, "Can't we all just get along." They praise the benefits of bipartisanship, which in their vernacular means we see and do things their way. But, and many will not want to hear this, there's a war going on—a spiritual war that will be won or lost, as opposed to being negotiated.

Christ said, "He who is not with Me is against Me, and he who does not gather with Me scatters abroad." (Matthew 12:30)

With that as the standard, we can see why He must be destroyed. God is not about negotiating. He commands His creations to obey Him.

But man, through arrogance, no longer believes in God's loving care. "Man is god," Progressives shout. The ascendancy of man has eclipsed the outdated notion and foolishness of God. Christianity is hokum, believed only by fools.

Sadly, as a society, we look at history and learn nothing. The same Progressive ideology of hundreds of years, which has failed again and again, is still being peddled as forward "Progressive" thinking. In fact, it shows the inability of man to govern himself. All the world's problems are a result of man failing to listen to God.

How do you kill God? You don't - You kill his children. It's the *Puff-the-Magic-Dragon* principle.

Once his friend (Jackie) no longer believed in him, Puff ceased to exist. Again, no comparison here, focus on the principle. Or let me put it another way: if a king has no subjects, is he still a king? If a father loses his children, is he still a father? We, the children of God, who still worship and obey Him, are being destroyed in order to "kill" Him, because He stands in the way of total domination of the masses by the hedonistic ruling elite.

How far has the Left come? They are so emboldened now that people like Nancy Pelosi openly masquerade as a Christian, while championing the "right" of a woman to an abortion, even late-term. Worse than her hypocrisy is the ineffectual church that allows her membership and the right of sacrament. That's how perverse things have become. The battle is almost over.

Now go back to the bible of the Progressives (*Rules for Radicals*) and apply the rules we discussed, not in a political light, but a spiritual one. Are not Christian leaders forced to capitulate or be made fun of?

Are those who still stand for God singled out and diminished as being out-of-touch, far right? Are we not under constant pressure and scrutiny for our stand against abortion? Isn't our Bible used against us at every turn?

It doesn't make a whit of difference what the subject is, the principles of *Rule for Radicals*, a book more or less devoted to socialist ideology, has been fine-tuned to be used against Christians, the last hope of the world. And they have been most successful in a very short period of time.

Anyone my age can tell you that—in a sense—time is being compressed by Progressives. What was unthinkable just a few decades ago is now the "new normal." What is abhorrent in one generation is tolerated in the next and embraced in the next. At the speed we're heading, the battle will be over shortly. We will either be ruled by a loving God, who gave His only Son so we can experience everlasting life, or by the lowest of men who believe, at every level, that they should be worshipped, for that is the right of royalty.

> "No one can serve two masters; for either he will hate the one
> and love the other, or else he will be loyal to the one and despise
> the other. You cannot serve God and mammon."
> (Matthew 6:24)

Couple this with Christ saying we are either with or against Him, and you see why there is *no* common ground. The Progressive Left knows that, which is why they are intent on destroying their spiritual opposition that they see through the eyes of a political animal. Unfortunately, Christians do not see the obvious.

From this point forward, I urge you to view current events, especially those that involve any spiritual matter, especially the church, with an understanding of the *Rule for Radicals*. If you do, it won't take long to see what's happening; it will all soon become painfully obvious that we're in a war we didn't even know we were in.

I study history for one reason.

That which has been [is] what will be, That which [is] done is what will be done, And [there is] nothing new under the sun. Ecclesiastes 1:9)

This battle has happened before, and we should learn from it, because this time it's personal and for keeps; America is the world's last great hope, and therefore *must* right the ship before it's too late. Darkness or light, that is our choice.

Do not be unequally yoked together with unbelievers. For what fellowship has righteousness with lawlessness? And what communion has light with darkness?
(2 Corinthians 6:14)

Speaking of history, and that the Progressives are trying to kill our God by destroying our faith, what is one of the first things every socialistic/communist government does once they gain political power? That's right, they outlaw religion, especially Christianity. Why? Because they know, just as the Bible says, their brand of government cannot coexist with God and His Son.

If you'll look around and be objective, the battle cannot be denied or ignored any longer. Progressives aren't just exposing their warped political views, they are in the process of killing God by destroying our collective faith. They will not stand for competition from anyone on any level. So they start at the top, with God.

In other countries, like Russia, China, Cuba, etc., when religion (Christianity) was outlawed, people routinely risked their lives to meet in basements under cover of darkness to worship our Lord. But in America, where religion has yet to be made illegal, hardly anyone shows up to church anymore. And if they do, it's too often at some mega-church that can live in harmony with the politicos—a church that goes along to get along. Certainly not one that challenges the status quo. A church that has a better gift shop, than sanctuary. God's Church and the churches of America, are, in general, no longer on the same page.

Church no longer influences our politics; politics influences our churches, and that's a dangerous sign.

How sad our Founding Fathers, most devote Christians, must be to see what has happened to their once-great vision inspired by the God they worshipped. How sad they must be to see the doctrine of the "separation of church and state" made up, and most certainly not part of our Constitution. For the record, the historical intention of the Framers was always to protect the church from the state. That truth has been perverted to now mean to most that we must somehow protect the state form the church. The entire intent of the Constitution, the basis of our constitutional republic, has been turned on its head. And since public schools no longer teach, but rather indoctrinate, generations of children have been taught the lie they now accept as truth. Our adversary has become our "friend," while our loving Father has become our "enemy."

I cannot overstate how important it is that we all become aware of what is unfolding in front of our eyes every day.

Once you become aware, you'll be stunned at how far the battle has progressed. It's a battle of attrition, and we're losing. Fewer and fewer people refer to themselves as Christians. Fewer still say they attend church regularly. This is not just happenstance; this is designed in stealth to reach an objective heretofore not thought possible—the killing of God.

Progressives know Christ is King, but on His return to earth (as he promised), they want to ensure He has no subjects. If that happens, He may still be King, but He will rule no one, which from the Left's point of view, will be delightfully ironic.

We are in no way confusing politics and religion here, for to the Progressive Left politics *is* their religion, and they are true believers.

Lastly, if you doubt the conclusions of this chapter, and therefore question the intent of the Progressives whose bible is *Rules for Radicals*, allow me to quote the dedication of Mr. Alinsky's tome: "Lest we forget at least an over-the-shoulder acknowledgment to the very first radical: from all our legends, mythology, and history... the first radical known to man who rebelled against the establishment and did it so effectively that he at least won his own kingdom — Lucifer."

4

FUSILLADING

A firing squad, also called fusillading, is used to inflict the ultimate in capital punishment. It's an old practice, usually thought of and used in a time of war for treason. Bows and arrows were used before the advent of firearms.

"JERUSALEM – Some have been taking issue with largely unnoticed comments made last year by Sen. Barack Obama declaring the U.S. is 'no longer a Christian nation,' but is also a nation of others, including Muslims and nonbelievers.

The comments have been recently recirculating on Internet blogs.

'Whatever we once were, we're no longer a Christian nation. At least not just. We are also a Jewish nation, a Muslim nation, and a Buddhist nation, and a Hindu nation, and a nation of nonbelievers,'

(Obama said during a June 2007 speech available on YouTube).

At the speech, Obama also seemingly blasted the 'Christian Right' for hijacking religion and using it to divide the nation:

'Somehow, somewhere along the way, faith stopped being used to bring us together and started being used to drive us apart. It got hijacked. Part of it's because of the so-called leaders of the Christian Right, who've been all too eager to exploit what divides us,' he said.

Asked last year to clarify his remarks, Obama repeated them to the Christian Broadcast Network:

'I think that the right might worry a bit more about the dangers of sectarianism. Whatever we once were, we're no longer just a Christian nation; we are also a Jewish nation, a Muslim nation, a Buddhist nation, a Hindu nation, and a nation of nonbelievers,' Obama wrote 'We should acknowledge this and realize that when we're formulating policies from the state house to the Senate floor to the White House, we've got to work to translate our reasoning into values that are accessible to every one of our citizens, not just members of our own faith community,' wrote Obama."

(In an e-mail to CBN News senior national correspondent David Brody) (www.WND.com Published: 06/22/2008 at 6:50 PM)

On January 20, 2009, Sen Barak Hussein Obama was inaugurated the 44th President of the United States of America.

On April 30, 1789 George Washington was inaugurated America's first president. The following quote is from his farewell address.

"The name of American, which belongs to you in your national capacity, must always exalt the just pride of patriotism more than any appellation derived from local discrimination's. With slight shades of difference, you have the same religion, manners, habits, and political principles. ...Of all the dispositions and habits, which lead to political prosperity, religion and morality are indispensable supports. In vain would that man claim the tribute of patriotism, who should labor to subvert these great pillars of human happiness, these firmest props of the duties of men and citizens. The mere politician, equally with the pious man, ought to respect and to cherish them. A volume could not trace all their connections with private and public felicity. Let it simply be asked: Where is the security for property, for reputation, for life, if the sense of religious obligation desert the oaths, which are the instruments of investigation in courts of justice? And let us with caution indulge the supposition that morality can be maintained without religion.

Whatever may be conceded to the influence of refined education on minds of peculiar structure, reason and experience both forbid us to expect that national morality can prevail in exclusion of religious principle."
(Washington's farewell address: Library of Congress)

He also wrote:

"You do well to wish to learn our arts and ways of life, and above all, the religion of Jesus Christ. These will make you a greater and happier people than you are. Congress will do every thing they can to assist you in this wise intention; and to tie the knot of friendship and union so fast, that nothing shall ever be able to loose it."
(George Washington speech to the Delaware Indian Chiefs (May 12, 1779); published in *The Writings of George Washington* (1932), Vol. XV, p. 55)

If you doubted how far we have fallen, the comparisons from our first-elected president to the 44th should put your doubts to rest. We are no longer the same, and we have not changed for the better. We are a secular nation.

Again, I know I am older than most, but I tell you the truth when I say that if Barak Obama was running for office 20 years ago and said what he said in Jerusalem in 2007, he could not have been elected. He wouldn't even have been nominated.

By the way, I want to refer you to what President Obama said about the "Religious Right" as it's a perfect example of what we talked about last chapter. What he said is exactly what the secular Left does (divisive politics), so he preemptively accused the Right of using the tactic of the Left. Then he singled out (isolated) the Right - not the Left, not Muslims, not non-believers. And while we're at it, when's the last time you heard anyone, even those on "our" side use the term Secular Left? We are always referred to as the "Radical Right," while they are referred to as "mainstream America."

Quickly, I want to use a few additional quotes to make my point that we're on a path that as a nation was never intended.

"The general principles upon which the [Founding] Fathers achieved independence were the general principals of Christianity..."
(John Adams)

"This is all the inheritance I give to my dear family. The religion of Christ will give them one which will make them rich indeed"
(John Henry)

"The Congress of the United States recommends and approves the Holy Bible for use in all schools." (Congress) [N.B. The Constitution was written in 1787]

"The United States of America were no longer Colonies. They were an independent nation of Christians"
(John Quincy Adams)
[John Quincy Adams was not one of the original founding fathers]

There are literally hundreds, if not more, such comments made by those who had the strength of faith to build this country, it's not necessary to name them all. I would, however, like to have you read this prayer from the father of modern-day liberalism:

"My Fellow Americans:

Last night, when I spoke with you about the fall of Rome, I knew at that moment that troops of the United States and our Allies were crossing the Channel in another and greater operation. It has come to pass with success thus far.

And so, in this poignant hour, I ask you to join with me in prayer:

Almighty God: Our sons, pride of our nation, this day have set upon a mighty endeavor, a struggle to preserve our Republic, our religion, and our civilization, and to set free a suffering humanity.

Lead them straight and true; give strength to their arms, stoutness to their hearts, steadfastness in their faith.

They will need Thy blessings. Their road will be long and hard. For the enemy is strong. He may hurl back our forces. Success may not come with rushing speed, but we shall return again and again; and we know that by Thy grace, and by the righteousness of our cause, our sons will triumph.

They will be sore tried, by night and by day, without rest—until the victory is won. The darkness will be rent by noise and flame. Men's souls will be shaken with the violences of war.

For these men are lately drawn from the ways of peace. They fight not for the lust of conquest. They fight to end conquest. They fight to liberate. They fight to let justice arise, and tolerance and goodwill among all Thy people. They yearn but for the end of battle, for their return to the haven of home.

Some will never return. Embrace these, Father, and receive them, Thy heroic servants, into Thy kingdom.

And for us at home -- fathers, mothers, children, wives, sisters, and brothers of brave men overseas, whose thoughts and prayers are ever with them -- help us, Almighty God, to re-dedicate ourselves in renewed faith in Thee in this hour of great sacrifice.

Many people have urged that I call the nation into a single day of special prayer. But because the road is long and the desire is great, I ask that our people devote themselves in a continuance of prayer. As we rise to each new day, and again when each day is spent, let words of prayer be on our lips, invoking Thy help to our efforts.

Give us strength, too—strength in our daily tasks, to redouble the contributions we make in the physical and the material support of our armed forces.

And let our hearts be stout, to wait out the long travail, to bear sorrows that may come, to impart our courage unto our sons wheresoever they may be.

And, O Lord, give us faith. Give us faith in Thee; faith in our sons; faith in each other; faith in our united crusade. Let not the keenness of our spirit ever be dulled. Let not the impacts of temporary events, of temporal matters of but fleeting moment—let not these deter us in our unconquerable purpose.

With Thy blessing, we shall prevail over the unholy forces of our enemy. Help us to conquer the apostles of greed and racial arrogances. Lead us to the saving of our country, and with our sister nations into a world unity that will spell a sure peace -- a peace invulnerable to the schemings of unworthy men. And a peace that will let all of men live in freedom, reaping the just rewards of their honest toil.

Thy will be done, Almighty God."

Amen.
(President Franklin D. Roosevelt - June 6, 1944)

How can anyone read the President's speech and not see that he believed we were a Christian nation. He was our 32nd president.

Presidents throughout history have always acknowledged the unique relationship America has had with God, right up to, but not including Barak Obama. He is a secular president, with policies almost always in conflict with the Word of God.

From the father of the modern Left, President Roosevelt, to the father of the modern Conservative movement, Ronald Reagan—

"We stand together as we did two centuries One people under God determined that our future shall be worthy of our past." (President Ronald Reagan, Jan. 21, 1985)

America has always been proud to say it was a Christian nation - but no more. Our President has severed the relationship and in the process done immeasurable harm to our nation. We have gone from being blessed by God to being His enemy, and we will pay a price for that choice.

Do you not know that friendship with the world is enmity with God? Whoever therefore wants to be a friend of the world makes himself an enemy of God.
(James 4:4)

There are now so many other enemies of God in America that it would be impossible and boring to name them all, but a few are worthy of note.

Atheists

Atheists, once individuals who refused to believe in God, were individuals without political purpose, but that has changed. The following is from the American Atheists web page (www.atheists.org):

"Since 1963, American Atheists has been the premier organization fighting for the civil liberties of atheists and the total, absolute separation of government and religion. American Atheists was born out of a court case begun in 1959 by the Murray family, which challenged prayer recitation in the public schools.

That case, Murray v. Curlett, was a landmark in American jurisprudence on behalf of our First Amendment rights. It began:

"Your petitioners are atheists, and they define their lifestyle as follows. An atheist loves himself and his fellow man instead of a god. An atheist accepts that heaven is something for which we should work now

– here on earth – for all men together to enjoy. An atheist accepts that he can get no help through prayer, but that he must find in himself the inner conviction and strength to meet life, to grapple with it, to subdue it and to enjoy it. An atheist accepts that only in a knowledge of himself and a knowledge of his fellow man can he find the understanding that will help lead to a life of fulfillment."

Now in its 50th year, American Atheists is dedicated to working for the civil rights of atheists, promoting separation of state and church, and providing information about atheism. Over the last fifty years, American Atheists has:

- Fought fervently to defend the separation of religion from government
- Appeared in all forms of media to defend our positions and criticisms of religion and mythology
- Held atheist conventions and gatherings throughout the United States, including "Atheist Pride" marches in state capitals
- Demonstrated and picketed throughout the country on behalf of atheist rights and state/church separation
- Published hundreds of books about atheism, criticism of religion, and state/church separation
- Published newsletters, magazines, and member alerts
- Built a robust and diverse community of local affiliates, partners, and activists
- Fostered a growing network of representatives throughout the nation who monitor important First Amendment issues and work on behalf of the organization in their areas
- Grown a network of volunteers who perform a variety of important tasks in their community, from placing American Atheist books in libraries to writing letters and publicizing the atheist perspective
- Preserved atheist literature and history in the nation's largest archive of its kind. The library's holdings span over three-hundred years of atheist thought.

- Provided speakers for colleges, universities, clubs, and the news media
- Granted college scholarships to young atheist activists"

The ACLU

The American Civil Liberties Union issued the following press release, and although it is just one case in their attempt to remove God from our society, it shows that they will leave no stone unturned; e.g., they want Christian grave markers removed from cemeteries (like Arlington National Cemetery) that honor those, who served this country with the ultimate sacrifice.

March 24, 2004

FOR IMMEDIATE RELEASE

"WASHINGTON - The American Civil Liberties Union today urged the Supreme Court to uphold a federal appeals court ruling that public schools are constitutionally barred from linking patriotism and piety by reciting the phrase "under God" as part of the Pledge of Allegiance.

"The government should not be asking impressionable schoolchildren to affirm their allegiance to God at the same time that they are affirming their allegiance to the country," said ACLU Legal Director Steven R. Shapiro.

"Removing 'under God' from the Pledge is not anti-religious," he added. "Just the opposite is true. The only way the religious reference in the Pledge can be upheld is for the Court to conclude that the words 'under God' have no religious meaning, which is far more insulting to people of faith."

As the ACLU noted in a friend-of-the-court brief, Congress added the phrase "under God" at the height of the anti-communist McCarthy Era. In signing the bill, then-President Eisenhower said that the phrase "under God" was added so that schoolchildren would 'daily proclaim' the dedication of our nation and our people to the Almighty."

The case, Elk Grove Unified School District v. Newdow, 02-1624, was originally brought by a California man, Michael Newdow, against his daughter's public-school district, where children as young as five are asked to recite the Pledge. Newdow argued that the district's Pledge- of-Allegiance policy directly interfered with his parental right to influence his daughter's religious development and, at the same time violated the Constitution's prohibition against government entanglement with religion. He is arguing the case today in the Supreme Court.

While the government has insisted that the Pledge is simply an "acknowledgment" of this country's religious heritage, the ACLU's Supreme Court brief cited social science research demonstrating that many children perceive the words "under God" as a form of prayer.

Indeed, President Bush has said much the same thing. In a November 2002 letter to Hawaiian religious leaders that is attached as an appendix to the ACLU brief, President Bush wrote:

"When we pledge allegiance to One Nation under God, our citizens participate in an important American tradition of humbly seeking the wisdom and blessing of Divine Providence."

In its 2002 ruling striking down the phrase, the Ninth Circuit Court of Appeals found that "a profession that we are a nation 'under God' is identical, for Establishment Clause purposes, to a profession that we are a nation 'under Jesus,' a nation 'under Vishnu,' a nation 'under Zeus,' or a nation 'under no god,' because none of these professions can be neutral with respect to religion." The appeals court added that the coercive effect of this policy is "particularly pronounced in the school setting given the age and impressionability of schoolchildren."

Justice Antonin Scalia, who had earlier criticized the appeals court's decision in the Pledge case, has recused himself from ruling in today's case. Therefore, the Ninth Circuit decision will stand in the event of a 4-4 split.

Joining the ACLU in its friend-of-the-court brief are Americans United for Separation of Church and State and Americans for Religious Liberty. The Court has received almost 50 friend-of-the-court briefs in the case, representing the broad range of opinion on this controversial issue."

(Copyright 2004 American Civil Liberties Union. Originally posted by the ACLU at https://www.aclu.org/content/aclu-urges-supreme-court-uphold-ruling-removing-phrase-under-god-pledge-allegiance-recited-p.)

Radical Feminists

Radical feminists have joined the ranks too, which is to me particularly disturbing as there was a time I was in-tune with their original objectives. For example, how could anyone believe it was right that two people doing the exact same job (at the same skill level) should not be paid the same? But commonsense objectives like that long ago were scrapped. We've long since left the National Organization of Women, as radical as it had become, and are now into a whole new branch of radical feminists, who openly and proudly oppose God.

On June 28, 2012, Secular Woman Inc made its debut as the first organization for atheist, humanist, and other non-religious women. The organization's vision is:

"…a future in which women without supernatural beliefs have the opportunities and resources they need to participate openly and confidently as respected voices of leadership in the secular community and every aspect of American society."

"With this organization we plan to focus on promoting the secular female voice, but anyone who supports our mission can join," said Bridget Gaudette. "All are vital to the success of Secular Woman and to the overall secular movement."

The leaders and co-founders of the organization are Brandi Braschler, Vice President of Programs; Bridget Gaudette, Vice President of Outreach; and Mary Ellen Sikes, Vice President of Operations. These four women make up the board of directors and bring more than 40 years of Secular and women's rights activism experience to the organization.

The organization's programs deal with advocacy, awards, grants, and various secular women's stories, along with "strategic partnerships," such as the National Council of Women's Organizations.

The Secular Woman Inc is a non-profit organization, and its mission is to "amplify the voice, presence, and influence of non-religious women."

Their **values** embrace humanism.

- We embrace human-centered ethics informed by reason and science. We reject dogma, superstition, pseudoscience, and religious authority as sources of morality and truth.
- We hold that all human beings are entitled to freedom from others' religious ideologies in living their lives, engaging with service providers, and interacting with government.
- They value health and sexuality.
- We support every person's right to bodily and sexual autonomy. Gender expression, sexual orientation, and matters of intimacy are for individuals to determine.
- We view age-appropriate, comprehensive, medically accurate health and sex education as vital to responsible decision-making by young people.
- We oppose all attempts to criminalize or limit access to comprehensive reproductive services such as contraception and abortion.
- We affirm that everyone has the right to feel safe, confident, and secure in their personal and emotional interactions. We oppose harassment, bullying, objectification, and other forms of aggression both physical and non-physical in all settings.

They also value family and relationships, feminism, and Secular community. They abhor the use of religion to suppress women, insisting that women have basic human rights equal to that of men.

Through strategic partnerships, Secular Woman will also advocate for equal pay, reproductive choice, and marriage equality, addressing political trends the group sees as ideologically-motivated threats to its members' freedom of conscience. "The 'War on Women' dovetailing with the rise of secular activism showed us the time had come for secular women to form our own distinct organization to support our vision of the future," said Kim Rippere, a Secular Woman founder and the organization's first president. "Secular women have always been at front and center of the feminist quest for equality and autonomy."

They offer various resources for women, including a database of Secular organizations, which establish anti-harassment policies, and offer speakers for various events.

The organization also offers a Secular Woman's Chronicle, published twice daily, and provides a blog for members." (source: www.goddiscussion.com) & (www.secularwomen.org)

Lawyers

The court system of America no longer reflects justice, but a system by lawyers for lawyers. And since most lawyers are uber-liberal, having been taught at law schools (especially in the east) that have at their helm the radical liberals of the 1960s, they too have a liberal agenda that doesn't include God. In fact, and I'm trying to be fair, most lawyers (who also happen to control our Congress) are a reflection of the old joke, What's the difference between a lawyer and God? God doesn't think He's a lawyer.

The following are just a few cases that reveal the trend of the courts at all levels to expunge God and His teachings from our declining society.

1962, *Engel v. Vitale*; Supreme Court finds prayer in schools unconstitutional.

1963, *Abington v. Schempp*; Supreme Court rules that Bible reading in public schools is unconstitutional.

1973, *Roe v. Wade*; Supreme court finds that the right to personal privacy includes infanticide.

1980, *Stone v. Graham*; Supreme court strikes down a Kentucky statute requiring display of the Ten Commandments in public schools.

2002, *Newdow v. U.S.*; 9th Circuit Court of Appeals rules that reciting "under God" in the Pledge of Allegiance in public schools is an unconstitutional endorsement of religion.

2003, *Lawrence v. Texas*; Supreme Court strikes down a Texas law prohibiting sodomy.

2003, *Glassroth v. Moore*; 11th Circuit Court of Appeals rules that a monument to the Ten Commandments placed in Alabama's judiciary building must be removed.

2003, *Goodridge v. Department of Public Health*; Massachusetts Supreme Court rules that same-sex couples can marry under the laws of that state.

2004, Massachusetts Supreme Court sanctions same-sex marriage; it declares that the state legislature may not offer "civil union" as an alternative to same-sex marriage, paving the way for the first state-recognized homosexual marriages in U.S. history.

2005, *U.S. v. Extreme Associates*; a U.S. district court judge dismisses federal obscenity charges against hardcore pornographers, finding that morality is no longer a legitimate state interest. (www.mission-toisrael.org)

Public School Teachers

America's public school system has become an arm of the "get God" crowd, which is alarming dangerous as they "teach" our children and direct their lives away from our religious teachings at home. Teachers have no problem with going against the wishes of parents as they know they will be upheld by their partners-in-crime, the courts. Actually, an objective review suggests that schools, especially colleges, no longer teach, but indoctrinate.

Sadly today's teachers' unions have been living off the reputation of past teachers, who were truly dedicated and deserving of respect. But today, to most teachers, teaching is not a calling, but rather a union job where the bottom-line is always about money and perks.

Which is why I get sick every time I hear a teacher's union president whose union is on strike say, "This isn't about the money; it's about the children!" Yet they never go on strike for better books, longer hours, a 12-month curricula, or anything that actually helps the kids. No, it's always, and I mean always, about their salaries that allows them 12 months of salary for 9 months work.

My feelings regarding teachers' unions are not mine alone. Here's a portion of an article from a Texas teacher.

"I have no real set opinion on teacher unions. This is mostly because I teach in Texas, where there is no teacher union, so I have no personal experience being a part of one. I finally got around to watching *Waiting for Superman,* a documentary critical of teacher unions, which went so far as to portray them as the cause of the educational slump in America. This may or may not be the case. While the film raised some good points it may have overstepped its bounds in some other areas. You can read an appropriate review of the film here.

Whatever your opinion of teachers unions, these demonstrations in Wisconsin seem a bit uncouth. Teachers calling in sick to protest and shutting down schools due to lack of available personnel seems equivalent to holding students hostage in order to make a point. Maybe the teachers protesting feel they are really helping students in the long run by taking this stand, but I don't think they can argue that they are doing anything but hurting the students now.

I firmly believe that if you are following God's calling for your life, it will most likely involve the forgoing of certain "rights" for the benefit of others. I also believe this is especially true in teaching. While I do not grasp all the details that have brought these protests about, it does seem like these teachers could have handled the situation in a more respectful manner.

(The State of Wisconsin and Texas: Please Pray by Josh Wilkerson www.godandmath.com/tag/teacher-unions)

Teachers, again having been part of the raucous 1960s or taught by left-leaning radicals from the same period, are, in general, not beholden to any form of discipline. They believe the teachings of Dr. Spock, the father of permissive parenting. They believe children should be allowed to "express themselves." That somewhat arguable thought ignores the "camel's nose under the tent" reality, and over decades that want of free expression turned into anarchy in the halls of most schools. The end result being that many teachers are deathly afraid of the students, and when you're afraid of the "children" your ability to teach is totally negated. The inmates are indeed running the asylum. That's what permissiveness does - always. Why?

Because it's in conflict with the Word of God.

He who spares his rod hates his son, But he who loves him disciplines him promptly.
(Proverbs 13:24)

Many people believe Proverbs 13:24 reads, "Spare the rod and spoil the child," which it obviously does not. The part that's left out is that those who spare the rod *hates his son*. Those are pretty hard words and completely change the meaning normally associated with the verse. God says those who are Progressively permissive with children "hate them." Remember that the next time a teacher's union president is stating how everything they do is for the kids, and then compare the complete lack of discipline in schools, originated by a new wave of teachers who know better than the millions of God-fearing teachers who preceded them. God says that we will be known by our fruits, and one of the fruits of teachers' unions reflects not love, but hate.

There are hundreds of groups that are being used by Satan, and/or are in willing consort, and there is no reason to name them all. The point is, once you get past their facades you'll see they aim to destroy our way of life…and to do that they must kill God, because He wants to save us at all costs, which is why He gave His Son to pay for our spiritual shortcomings.

Yes, God has many enemies. Some are obvious; some are not. It is up to us to watch and judge—not people, but events. Start listening to the leaders of various organizations, and then turn to your Bible. Compare and contrast, and you'll see a pattern, one most will never see until it's too late.

> Have you ever read the fable about the frog and the scorpion? A scorpion and a frog meet on the bank of a stream, and the scorpion asks the frog to carry him across on its back. The frog asks, "How do I know you won't sting me?" The scorpion says, "Because if I do, I will die too."
> The frog is satisfied, and they set out, but in midstream, the scorpion stings the frog. The frog feels the onset of paralysis and starts to sink, knowing they both will drown, but has just enough time to gasp "Why?"
> Replies the scorpion: "It's my nature..."
> (http://www.aesopfables.com)

Like the scorpion, man, non-Christian man, is who he is. It comes with our God-given free will. And the further down the road we get historically, the more rebellious we become. We don't need God. In fact, if it wasn't for God and all His stupid rules, man could really make some headway. Progressive groups don't believe in God, because to them, they are God. That's why they have policies that seek to make America heaven on earth, because they don't believe in the real heaven. That's why we have an ever-expanding welfare system; God isn't the fountainhead of our bounty, government is. This subject in particular, welfare, is a perfect example that God and the Progressives cannot coexist. Washington says that they will provide food, housing, clothes for whoever applies, even lawbreakers who cross our boarders illegally. God says:

> "For even when we were with you, we commanded you this: If anyone will not work, neither shall he eat."
> (2 Thessalonians 3:10)

Have I helped you see the enemy clearly now?

Actually, I've done nothing of the kind, as God's obvious enemies are not the ones who will kill Him. Christians will.

The truth is, as powerful as God's enemies are, they are powerless against Him. It is only through us, those who claim His name, can their work come to fruition. And we're letting them do it! Each day they take a step forward and we, God's children, take two steps back. Remember now, God's earthly enemies can only destroy Him by destroying our faith, so every time we go along to get along we, in effect, take the scourge from the Roman soldier's hand and administer another lash to the back of our Savior.

We, His family, are the enemy that will administer the death blow. Have doubts? Read Matthew 10:36, "And 'a man's enemies will be those of his [own] household." Are we not God's family? Then we are His true enemy, as we are the ones who can deal Him the most grief and misery.

Reading the Bible contextually makes clear that we give praise and worship, but we all too often refuse to give obedience.

"Not everyone who says to Me, 'Lord, Lord,' shall enter the kingdom of heaven, but he who does the will of My Father in heaven. (Matthew 7:21)

"But why do you call Me 'Lord, Lord,' and not do the things which I say? (Luke 6:46)

They profess to know God, but in works they deny [Him], being abominable, disobedient, and disqualified for every good work. (Titus 1:16)

The point is, God's obvious enemies are not the problem. We are!

We're the ones who have turned from God's Word and allowed Liberals to replace it with political correctness. We're the ones who have stood silent as prayer was removed from schools. We haven't fought back in His holy name while righteous discipline was replaced with a permissive teaching culture that is destroying the moral fiber of the children entrusted to their care. We applauded as radical feminists have made Colossians 3:18, "Wives, submit to your own husbands, as is fitting in the Lord," into a joke, and something to be avoided. We say nothing as court after court strikes down the Christian underpinnings of our nation, while secular judges sit under the motto "In God We Trust." We've watched and done nothing as the homosexual agenda turned from securing human dignity for all into an active agenda that places deviant sexual practices above God. We've said nothing as marriage is no longer what God intended, but rather reflects the lowest common denominator. We've sat in mute silence and fear while "mothers" aborted over 50 million innocent souls who God says He knew before they were born. We've participated in adulteries and then remarried our 2nd, 3rd, or 4th wife - and the church says nothing, notwithstanding God says marriage is until death. There are so many issues, and our side is losing them all, because we will not stand with Him. To do so is sometimes costly and most often embarrassing.

But it's all right, as we believe we have an "out."

Here's another interesting aspect about fusillading. Sometimes one or more members of the firing squad are issued a weapon containing a blank cartridge instead of a live round. No member of the firing squad is told ahead of time if he is using a blank or live ammunition. This is reinforces the sense of diffusion of responsibility among the firing squad members, making the execution process more reliable by removing any human hesitancy. It also allows members of the firing squad to believe that he did not personally fire a fatal shot—this is sometimes referred to as the conscience round.

That's what we Christians do - we have become incredible shrinking violets, never openly standing for the Lord, and then take comfort in the fact that we're not openly working against Him. It's our spiritual "conscience round."

We feel as long as we go to church, we're okay. But if that's all we do in His name, the world then sees Christians as seculars who happen to go to church on Sunday. Nothing more.

When's the last time you witnessed for Christ? Spoke His name at work? Corrected someone when they were in clear violation of what God asks of us? Do you look the other way, when you know in your heart you shouldn't?

Over the last twenty years a new form of Christianity has emerged. I, and others, call its practitioners "worldly Christians." As I mentioned, the only difference between those who now profess to be followers of Christ and unbelievers is the "Christians" go to church. In every other way they are alike. The new church hierarchy tells us we are to get along with the outside world, and how important it is that we are accepted, and when we talk about Christian living we're doing harm to the church, as then society sees us as a "buzz kill." A bunch of arrogant legalists. It used to be that our guide for life was the Bible; now we're afraid to leave a Bible out in the house lest a guest see it and think ill of us. And by falling short we leave our children to fend for themselves, as they learn from us to hide their faith. That's why so many follow the hip-hop culture while eschewing decent Christian living. That's why so many children dress as they have no respect for anyone, including themselves.

We're afraid to speak up regarding sex before marriage, notwithstanding that the Bible says the unrepentant fornicators will not set foot in heaven. No, the prevailing attitude is, "kids are going to have sex anyway, so we have to help them do it safely." First of all, if this theory worked, we wouldn't have the illegitimate birth rate we have today. But over and above the obvious, please tell me what's so safe about relegating one's self to hell, because unless we repent that's what's going to happen. The question then must be asked, who are we worshipping? God, who says no to premarital sex, or society that says yes? This is another subject where you can see society's application of the *Rules for Radicals* being applied to Christians who try and preach abstinence; they are openly ridiculed and marginalized.

Have you ever wondered why evil is represented by darkness and the Lord by light?

Ask yourself, when does most sin occur? Satan does his dirty work behind closed doors, in secret, while God deals openly and honestly in the light of day, as He has nothing to hide. He is honest. And we are to reflect the character of the One we say we worship. But most of us don't. We look away from the sex scandals of our political leaders. We say it doesn't matter what a person does behind closed doors, even if it's an adultery, as long as he/she is a good "leader." This is the new normal of the Progressives. Character doesn't matter, and in the process the character of the nation is equal to the character of a slug. Again, we cannot blame the morally inept politicians, but ourselves, as we elect them, watch them embarrass the nation, and then vote them into office yet again.

I am reminded so often of the synergy between the Bible and the advice from Edmund Burke - "All that is necessary for the triumph of evil is that good men do nothing."

God's enemies, those who wish Him dead, are only as successful as we (Christians) allow them to be. It's time for us to wake up! It is critical for us to get our house in order!

The battle is like a candle burning. With each passing minute the light of the Lord gets dimmer and dimmer until, soon, we will have nothing left but the darkness of evil - and we will have no one to blame but ourselves.

Are you living like a saint or an unabashed sinner who simply calls himself a Christian?

Nevertheless the solid foundation of God stands, having this seal: "The Lord knows those who are His," and, "Let everyone who names the name of Christ depart from iniquity." But in a great house there are not only vessels of gold and silver, but also of wood and clay, some for honor and some for dishonor. Therefore if anyone cleanses himself from the latter, he will be a vessel for honor, sanctified and useful for the Master, prepared for every good work. Flee also youthful lusts; but pursue righteousness, faith, love, peace with those who call on the Lord out of a pure heart. (2 Timothy 2:19-22)

Like it or not, the Bible says those masquerading as Christians are of no use to God. There is a clear bright line of discipleship. Are you, as one who claims His name, willing to die for Him as the disciples did? If not, your claim to be a Christian is false.

And churches? They are perhaps the worse as they lead more and more children to their spiritual destruction. The church used to be the one entity that would stand for Christ no matter what. Now we have nuns and female church members marching for a woman's right to choose (kill her baby)

Some churches welcome practicing homosexuals instead of separating from them as the Bible commands.Some churches, instead of standing strong, cover-up sexual wrongdoing by the church hierarchy. And if young couples want to live together and/or have children without benefit of marriage, no problem, our doors are open for everyone. And most churches have no trouble with adultery and/or remarriage, notwithstanding that the Bible makes clear that God hates divorce and marriage is until one partner passes.

The pious, who want to use and twist Christ's words and intentions (part of the *Rules for Radicals*) will say that church is not a home for saints, but a hospital for sinners. That sounds good, but it's not true.

In the name of our Lord Jesus Christ, when you are gathered together, along with my spirit, with the power of our Lord Jesus Christ, deliver such a one to Satan for the destruction of the flesh, that his spirit may be saved in the day of the Lord Jesus. Your glorying [is] not good.

Do you not know that a little leaven leavens the whole lump? Therefore purge out the old leaven, that you may be a new lump, since you truly are unleavened. For indeed Christ, our Passover, was sacrificed for us.

Therefore let us keep the feast, not with old leaven, neither with the leaven of malice and wickedness; but with the unleavened [bread] of sincerity and truth. I wrote unto you in an epistle not to company with fornicators: Yet not altogether with the fornicators of this world, or with the covetous, or extortioners, or with idolaters; for then must ye needs go out of the world.

But now I have written unto you not to keep company, if any man that is called a brother be a fornicator, or covetous, or an idolater, or a railer, or a drunkard, or an extortioner; with such an one no not to eat.

For what have I to do to judge them also that are without? Do not ye judge them that are within? But them that are without God judgeth. Therefore put away from among yourselves that wicked person.
(1 Corinthians 5:4-13)

We all fall short of the glory of God.
(Romans 3:23).

But there's a difference between sin we struggle with and sin we accept as part of our life, sin we have no intention of changing.

Sadly, far too many churches have capitulated to the pressures of society. So much so they sit in silence as our nation turns its back on God. Heaven forbid that they say anything "controversial," lest they lose their tax-exempt status with the Internal Revenue Service. And most clearly the argument about the separation between church and state has been lost, so why say anything? (Even though history makes absolutely clear the secular argument is false from top-to-bottom.)

Churches, not all, but most, are but a shell of their former selves. They are no longer the standard-bearer for Christ, but now a spiritual comfort-stop that gives nominal Christians and rebellious sinners comfort in their sins. This is how God will be killed. His children, as if in a bad novel, will be the vehicle to do what God's obvious enemies cannot do alone. We who are closest to His heart will stop it.

CONCLUSION

"*Is God Dead?*" was an April 8, 1966, cover story for the news magazine: *Time*. A previous article from October 1965 had investigated a trend among 1960s-theologians to write God out of the field of theology.

The 1966 article looked in greater depth at the problems facing modern theologians, in making God relevant to an increasingly secular society. Modern science had eliminated the need for religion to explain the natural world, and God took up less and less space in people's daily lives. The ideas of various scholars were brought in, including the application of contemporary philosophy to the field of theology, and a more personal, individual approach to religion." (Time. April 1966)

In 2009, Newsweek wrote, "America Has Moved Into A "Post-Christian" Phase "[God] Is Less Of A Force In American Politics And Culture Than At Any Other Time In Recent Memory" NEW YORK, April 5 /PRNewswire/

According to the new Newsweek Poll, fewer people now think of the United States as a "Christian nation" than did so when George W. Bush was president. Two thirds of the public now say religion is "losing influence" in American society, and the proportion of Americans who think religion "can answer all or most of today's problems" is now at a historic low of 48% .

Newsweek Editor Jon Meacham explores this issue in the April 13 cover: "The Decline and Fall of Christian America" (on newsstands Monday, April 6) According to the American Religious Identification

Survey, the percentage of self-identified Christians has fallen 10% since 1990, from 86% to 76%.

Meacham writes that these figures show that America has not only become less Christian, but has moved into a "post-Christian" phase. "This is not to say that the Christian God is dead," he writes, "but that he is less of a force in American politics and culture than at any other time in recent memory." (www.reuters.com)

One of the problems with America is that it doesn't function on the same clock the rest of the world does. We want what we want, and we want it now! The rest of the world sees things in decades, centuries. We're thinking we have to fight radical Islam in the immediate, while they see their "victory" coming in hundreds of years. The same with the Chinese Communists. So when "nothing happens" for a few years, we think the problem has been solved, while our opposition believes they are just that much further along in their inevitable conquest.

Look again at the quick synopses of the two articles on God in America. Hopefully you'll be shocked at the differences in just five short decades. The seculars, too, view things long term. They know they're winning. But they also know this—God cannot be killed, not in a spiritual sense. He is, always has been, and always will be.

But, as we are mere humans, all things have a beginning and end, and God, as He pertains to our society and us personally, is out of time. He is being tortured again, just as He was prior to the crucifixion.

"Jesus of Nazareth underwent Jewish and Roman trials, was flogged, and was sentenced to death by crucifixion. The scourging produced deep stripe-like lacerations and appreciable blood loss, and it probably set the stage for hypovolemic shock as evidenced by the fact that Jesus was too weakened to carry the crossbar (patibulum) to Golgotha. At the site of crucifixion his wrists were nailed to the patibulum, and after the patibulum was lifted onto the upright post (stipes) his feet were nailed to the stipes.

The major pathophysiologic effect of crucifixion was an interference with normal respiration. Accordingly death resulted primarily from hypovolemic shock and exhaustion asphyxia. Jesus' death was ensured by the thrust of a soldier's spear into his side. Modern medical interpretation of the historical evidence indicates that Jesus was dead when taken down from the cross." (JAMA 1986;255:1455-1463)

Virtually everything we do today is abusing our Lord and Savior and His Father. We've turned our backs on Him, just as the disciples did prior to the Resurrection. We, like them, talk a good game, but when it comes time to stand and be counted, we turn our backs and join the rebellious crowd intent on His destruction. We feel safer when we fit in.

Isn't that what we're doing when we do nothing to stop the slaughter of the unborn? When we divorce and remarry? When we harm our children by divorcing and separating? When we ignore His command regarding the proper relationship between husband and wife? When we cheer another victory for the radical homosexual agenda? When we lie and cheat without reservations or remorse? When we refuse to repent?

All our rebellions are lashes of the scourge to our loving God. His own children (the ones He sent His Son to die for so our sins could be forgiven and we could spend eternity in His presence) have shunned Him.

We don't want Him in our homes, our schools, our places of business, the cemeteries of those who paid the ultimate sacrifice for our country, our courts, our governments (at all levels), and, most sadly, our churches. We will do as we please.

God can only be killed from man's perspective, and that's what we're talking about. The job is almost complete. Yes, it may take decades or another thousand years. Who knows? But the path has been laid out by the seculars who, whether they know it or not, worship evil. And, as the saying goes, evil only triumphs when good men say and do nothing.

So which are you? Are you God's overt enemy?

Whoever therefore wants to be a friend of the world makes himself an enemy of God.
(James 4:4)

Or are you a fusillader, willing to fire, but not willing to admit what you've done, because there is a chance you fired the one blank in the firing squad?

Unsure of your spiritual status? There's an easy way to find out. Simply apply the biblical sentiment:

> Whoever therefore wants to be a friend of the world makes himself an enemy of God. Even so, every good tree bears good fruit, but a bad tree bears bad fruit. A good tree cannot bear bad fruit, nor [can] a bad tree bear good fruit. Every tree that does not bear good fruit is cut down and thrown into the fire. Therefore by their fruits you will know them.
> (Matthew 7:16-20).

Are you living for God or yourself? Will you speak His name in public? At work? Are you raising your children according to His Word? Are you faithful to Him? To your spouse and children? Are you watching things you shouldn't watch, drinking things you shouldn't drink? Are you hanging around with His enemies? These are the fruits of an unbeliever, no matter what you claim to those around you.

Or are you one, whom everyone knows is a child of God? One who speaks and stands for Him unabashedly.

For those in the process of killing God there is much bad news, as they can be successful in the here and now, but their objective in eternity is not possible, and they will pay a price for the choices they've made.

Everything in the Bible will come to pass. I believe it will happen sooner rather than later, as there are many signs that His return is close, and in the end we all will be judged.

As your brother in Christ Jesus, I beg you to turn from the foolishness of the secular to the rock-solid spiritual. Stop acting as if you don't care about God, or worse, that you don't care if He lives or dies.

He loves you with a love few can truly understand, such is its depth. He allowed His Son to be treated as we should be treated, so we could be treated like His Son. There is no greater love.

But make no mistake, we are in a war. It's good versus evil. You must choose sides. Remember what Jesus said:

He who is not with Me is against Me, and he who does not gather with Me scatters abroad.
(Matthew 12:30).

There is no longer any place to hide, and for those who think they can be non-committal by standing in the middle of the road, know this: people who stand in the middle of the road get run over.

Let no one deceive you with empty words, for because of these things the wrath of God comes upon the sons of disobedience.
(Ephesians 5:6).

Evil exists. So does good. Which do you choose? It doesn't matter what you say, only what you *do* will reveal who you worship.

Sadly, rendering ourselves voluntarily mute, which most of us do, is choosing evil. Goodness requires, by definition, being proactive.

Evil is trying to kill God by destroying His sheep, and by many measures Satan is becoming more successful by the day. But the Bible tells us that this story ends in God's victory. So in trying to kill God, we only kill ourselves and deny ourselves life everlasting.

God has always been, is, and always will be. He will not die no matter our efforts, but through our rebellion and/or silence we may become dead to Him.

As a minister I have yet to come to grips with the fact that so many of us choose everlasting torment in hell instead of the peace and love of heaven. The spiritual lunacy of that choice sometimes overwhelms me.

Let them not rejoice over me who are wrongfully my enemies;
Nor let them wink with the eye who hate me without a cause.
(Psalms 35:19)

POSTSCRIPT

I know there will be many who object to this book. There are the obvious enemies of God as we've discussed throughout. Then there are the not-so-obvious. Specifically, I'm referring to nominal Christians who are Christians in name only.

We all love the thought of a savior who saves us, but we rebel against the thought of a lord who requires discipleship and obedience. Therein lays the crux of the matter.

The Bible, the Word of God, constantly refers to Jesus as Lord *and* Savior. His love for us, based on His character and our response to the love He revealed on the Cross (obedience or disobedience) is a package-deal. If we will not let Jesus be our Lord, He will not be our Savior. We may worship a divided Christ, but if we do we are rightfully doomed.

> If anyone does not abide in Me, he is cast out as a branch and
> is withered; and they gather them and throw [them] into the
> fire, and they are burned.
> (John 15:6)

Christ preached the message of His Father, and yet many act as if they don't like what they hear.

Have I therefore become your enemy because I tell you the truth?
(Galatians 4:16)

Being on God's side isn't easy, and He wants us to know that before we commit.

Remember the word that I said to you, "A servant is not greater than his master.' If they persecuted Me, they will also persecute you. If they kept My word, they will keep yours also.
(John 15:20)

If we're having trouble choosing sides in the battle, understand this…being non-committal is choosing evil over good. "The darkest places in hell are reserved for those who maintain their neutrality in times of moral crisis." (Dante Alighieri)

You say you love God.

Greater love has no one than this, than to lay down one's life for his friends.
(John 15:13)

That's what the Son of God did for us on the Cross. Are you willing to do the same? So many of us are breaking God's loving heart.

We procrastinate while living in sin, always believing that we have time to see things God's way, that there's always tomorrow.

Here's another truth; most procrastinators die in their sin. For them, tomorrow never comes.

Whereas you do not know what [will happen] tomorrow. For what [is] your life? It is even a vapor that appears for a little time and then vanishes away.
(James 4:14)

(Commentary: Mathew 10:16-42) "Our Lord warned his disciples to prepare for persecution. They were to avoid all things, which gave advantage to their enemies, all meddling with worldly or political concerns, all appearance of evil or selfishness, and all underhand measures.

Christ foretold troubles, not only that the troubles might not be a surprise, but that they might confirm the hearers' faith. He tells them what they should suffer and from whom. Thus Christ has dealt fairly and faithfully with us, in telling us the worst we can meet with in his service; and he would have us deal so with ourselves, in sitting down and counting the cost.

Persecutors are worse than beasts, in that they prey upon those of their own kind. The strongest bonds of love and duty have often been broken through from enmity against Christ. Sufferings from friends and relations are very grievous; nothing cuts more.

It appears plainly, that all who will live godly in Christ Jesus must suffer persecution; and we must expect to enter into the kingdom of God through many tribulations. With these predictions of trouble, are counsels and comforts for a time of trial. The disciples of Christ are hated and persecuted as serpents, and their ruin is sought, and they need the serpent's wisdom.

Be ye harmless as doves. Not only, do nobody any hurt, but bear nobody any ill-will. Prudent care there must be, but not an anxious, perplexing thought; let this care be cast upon God.

The disciples of Christ must think more how to do well, than how to speak well. In case of great peril, the disciples of Christ may go out of the way of danger, though they must not go out of the way of duty.

No sinful, unlawful means may be used to escape; for then it is not a door of God's opening. The fear of man brings a snare, a perplexing snare, that disturbs our peace; an entangling snare, by which we are drawn into sin; and, therefore, it must be striven and prayed against. Tribulation, distress, and persecution cannot take away God's love to them, or theirs to him.

Fear Him, who is able to destroy both soul and body in hell. Christians must deliver their message publicly, for all are deeply concerned in the doctrine of the gospel. The whole counsel of God must be made known. See Acts 20:27.

Christ shows the disciples why they should be of good cheer. Their sufferings witnessed against those who oppose His gospel. When God calls us to speak for Him, we may depend on Him to teach us what to say. A believing prospect of the end of our troubles will be of great use to support us under them. They may be borne to the end, because the sufferers shall be borne up under them. The strength shall be according to the day.

That the work shall certainly be done is great encouragement to those who are doing Christ's work.

See how the care of Providence extends to all creatures, even to the sparrows. This should silence all the fears of God's people; Ye are of more value than many sparrows. And the very hairs of your head are all numbered. This denotes the account God takes and keeps of his people.

It is our duty, not only to believe in Christ, but to profess that faith, in suffering for him, when we are called to it, as well as in serving him. That denial of Christ only is here meant which is persisted in, and that confession only can have the blessed recompence here promised, which is the real and constant language of faith and love.

Religion is worth everything; all who believe the truth of it, will come up to the price, and make everything else yield to it. Christ will lead us through sufferings to glory with him. Those are best prepared for the life to come, who sit most loosely to this present life.

Though the kindness done to Christ's disciples be ever so small, yet if there be occasion for it, and ability to do no more, it shall be accepted. Christ does not say that they deserve a reward; for we cannot merit anything from the hand of God; but they shall receive a reward from the free gift of God. Let us boldly confess Christ, and show love to him in all things."   (http://biblehub.com/matthew/10-36.htm)

The road we are asked to travel in praise and worship is not an easy one. Perhaps that's why there are so few on that path anymore. Perhaps that's why we've invented a new user-friendly brand of Christianity.

One that requires no heavy lifting on our part. But that is denying Him.

> But whoever denies Me before men, him I will also deny before My Father who is in heaven.
> (Matthew 10:33)

The Wayfarer
Perceiving the pathway to truth,
Was struck with astonishment.
It was thickly grown with weeds.
"Ha," he said,
"I see that none has passed here
In a long time."
Later he saw that each weed
Was a singular knife.
"Well," he mumbled at last,
"Doubtless there are other roads."
(Stephen Crane)

Unlike the above poem's secular sentiment representing society's view of our obligations to God, consider the following:

> Jesus said to him, "I am the way, the truth, and the life. No one comes to the Father except through Me.
> (John 14:6)

How we react to God's love is an either/or proposition. It's good or evil: your choice. There is *no* middle ground. We are either with Him or against Him.

> As a minister of the Word of God, I cannot implore you strongly enough to choose sides. The time is now. God needs spiritual warriors who will fight those who are trying to kill Him.

Will you stand with Him?

Will you die for Him?

Will you speak His truth regardless of the consequences? And if you won't, what will you say on Judgment Day in your own defense?

But whosoever denies Me before men, him I will also deny before My Father who is in heaven.
(Matthew 10:33)

God has made clear what He expects from His children. Look into your heart. You know His truth.

And you shall know the truth, and the truth shall make you free.
(John 8:32)

The battle has begun.

> Onward, Christian soldiers, marching as to war,
> With the cross of Jesus going on before.
> Christ, the royal Master, leads against the foe;
> Forward into battle see His banners go!
>
> Refrain:
> Onward, Christian soldiers, marching as to war,
> With the cross of Jesus going on before.
>
> At the sign of triumph Satan's host doth flee;
> On then, Christian soldiers, on to victory!
> Hell's foundations quiver at the shout of praise;
> Brothers lift your voices, loud your anthems raise.
> Like a mighty army moves the church of God;
> Brothers, we are treading where the saints have trod.
> We are not divided, all one body we,
> One in hope and doctrine, one in charity.

Crowns and thrones may perish, kingdoms rise and wane,
But the church of Jesus constant will remain.
Gates of hell can never 'gainst that church prevail;
We have Christ's own promise, and that cannot fail.

Onward then, ye people, join our happy throng,
Blend with ours your voices in the triumph song.
Glory, laud, and honor unto Christ the King,
This through countless ages men and angels sing.

(Onward Christian Soldiers: Words written by Sabine Baring-Gould in 1865; music composed by Arthur Sullivan in 1871)

It's either good or evil, life or death, Christ or Satan. Please, I beg you, on bended knee, choose wisely. Choose knowing that staying silent is choosing evil, as a vote not cast is always a vote for the opposition.

Finally, my brethren, be strong in the Lord and in the power of His might. Put on the whole armor of God, that you may be able to stand against the wiles of the devil. For we do not wrestle against flesh and blood, but against principalities, against powers, against the rulers of the darkness of this age, against spiritual *hosts* of wickedness in the heavenly *places*.
(Ephesians 6:10-12)

Lastly, know this: Only those who stand for God in this life will stand with Him in the next.

OTHER BOOKS BY
EDWARD MRKVICKA

- ***THE GOSPEL OF "IF"*** (Crosslink Publishing - Fall 2013)
- ***THE SIN OF FORGIVENESS*** (Crosslink Publishing - Summer 2013)
  Winner NABE Pinnacle Book Achievement Award - Category: Religion
  Names FAPA President's Award Finalist - Category: Religion
- ***NO INNOCENT AFFAIR*** (Tate Publishing & Enterprises, Inc. -Sept. 2011)
  Named Books & Author's "Best Christian Book of the Year."
- ***THE PRAYER PROMISE OF CHRIST*** (Tate Publishing – Summer, 2010)
  Named "Best Christian Book of the Year" by Books & Authors. net.
- ***BE NOT DECEIVED*** (Trafford - 2007) Named "Best Christian Book of the Year," "Best Christian Study of the Year," was a National Book Awards Finalist (Religion/Christian), a Christian Choice Book Awards winner (category: "Bible Study"), and awarded the FaithWriters' Seal of Approval as an "Outstanding Read."

ABOUT THE AUTHOR

Dr. Edward Mrkvicka is a lay minister and counselor and life-long Bible student. His efforts on behalf of families have earned him a United States Certificate of Special Congressional Recognition "in recognition of outstanding and invaluable service to the community."

In 2012 he was awarded an Honorary Doctor of Divinity for "having served humanity as an author, lay minister, and counselor, with outstanding dedication to the sanctity of marriage and to God's Holy Church."

After serving in the Air Force from 1965-1969, he began his career in banking. By 1976 he was the youngest bank president in America.

After retiring in 1982 he opened Reliance Enterprises, Inc., a nationally known financial consulting firm.

During this time he also started his writing career by publishing:

- Battle Your Bank & Win! (William Morrow & Co.),
- Moving Up (William Morrow & Co),
- 1037 Ways To Make Or Save Up To$100,000 This Year Alone (Instant Improvement),
- The Rational Investor (Probus),
- The Bank Book (HarperCollins),
- Your Bank Is Ripping You Off (St. Martin's Press)
- Pick Winning Stocks (J.K. Lasser)

Most of his financial books have had numerous printings and editions. Some were award-winning, while others are used in college classrooms.

Through it all, Ed witnessed for his first love, Jesus. In fact, it was during his time in the military, while stationed on a Turkish Air Base, that he became a lay minister to his fellow servicemen. That ministry continues to this day.

Contacting the Author
Dr. Mrkvicka can be reached through his website:
www.edmrkvicka.com

Or write to him at:
PO Box 413
Marengo, IL 60152

Email: reliance1985@att.net.